Beyond *the* Noise

Your Guide to
Stock Research and Analysis

JENS VERBRUGGE

Copyright © 2025 All rights reserved.

ISBN: 9789083534800 (hardcover), 9789083534817 (paperback), 9789083534824 (e-book)
NUR: 794

No part of this publication may be copied, reproduced in any format, by any means, electronic or otherwise, without prior consent from the copyright owner and publisher of this book.

This book is intended for informational and educational purposes only and should not be considered financial, legal, or investment advice. While every effort has been made to provide accurate and useful insights, investing involves risk, and past performance is no guarantee of future results. Additionally, the market is constantly changing—stock prices, company situations, and economic conditions may have shifted since this book was written. Any examples provided are for illustration only and should not be interpreted as recommendations. Always conduct your own research and consult with a qualified financial professional before making any investment decisions.

To my beautiful wife, whom I never met.

Because I was too occupied analyzing stocks and acquiring the knowledge and experience for writing this book.

TABLE OF CONTENTS

PREFACE	1
CHAPTER 1: Why Invest?	3
CHAPTER 2: Investment Philosophies	13
CHAPTER 3: The Non-Efficient Market Hypothesis	25
CHAPTER 4: The Perfect Company	37
CHAPTER 5: Valuation	49
CHAPTER 6: M&A, Growth, and Capital Allocation	75
CHAPTER 7: Quality of the business	93
CHAPTER 8: Quality of the Sector & Region	107
CHAPTER 9: Quality of the Management	119
CHAPTER 10: The Other Shareholders	127
CHAPTER 11: When Should You Sell a Stock?	141
CHAPTER 12: Portfolio Construction	155
CHAPTER 13: How to Select a Fund?	161
CHAPTER 14: Closing Remarks	171
ACKNOWLEDGEMENTS	173

PREFACE

Welcome to *Beyond the Noise*. Congratulations! The fact that you are reading this book means you understand the needs and merits of equity investing, and the importance of research and analysis to become successful in this field.

While investing in stocks is one of the most rewarding ways to build wealth over time, for many, the stock market feels like a complex puzzle filled with jargon, unpredictable movements, and an overwhelming number of choices. This book is designed to help you navigate that world with clarity and confidence.

Whether you are a beginner looking to make your first investment or someone seeking to refine your stock research skills, my goal is to provide you with a toolbox of practical insights, proven techniques, and a mindset that fosters long-term success. Unlike passive investing, where you simply track an index, stock picking is about finding and investing in quality businesses at the right price. Done well, it can generate superior returns and help you take control of your financial future.

However, don't expect a "get rich quick" guide. Stock picking is not about chasing hype, acting on gut feelings, or making impulsive trades. It requires patience, research, and a solid understanding of how businesses create value. This book provides a structured approach to analyzing companies, identifying opportunities, managing risks, and avoiding common pitfalls that trip up even experienced investors.

While no one can predict the market's every move, a disciplined approach can significantly improve your odds of success.

I hope this book inspires you to think independently, make informed investment decisions, and approach stock picking with both curiosity and conviction. The stock market rewards those who are willing to do the work. Let's get started!

// PREFACE

About the Author

Jens Verbrugge is a seasoned equity portfolio manager and financial analyst at Value Square, a niche investment boutique specializing in long-term fundamental value investing.

Before joining Value Square, Jens spent a decade at a leading Belgian financial institution, first as a credit risk modeler, then as a quantitative equity investment analyst, refining his expertise in financial modelling and investment strategies.

He holds a master of engineering from Ghent University, and later expanded his financial acumen through a postgraduate degree in corporate finance. He is also a CFA charter holder.

Jens is passionate about uncovering undervalued opportunities in the stock market and helping investors navigate the complexities of stock picking with a structured and rational approach.

CHAPTER 1

Why Invest?

"Compound interest is the eighth wonder of the world. He who understands it, earns it...he who doesn't, pays it."

– ALBERT EINSTEIN

Don't let the cookie shrink

Lots of people feel overwhelmed when faced with investing decisions, so they leave their money in cash or savings. What they don't realize is that *not investing is actually making an investment decision*. Your cash is also an asset class, and with inflation constantly nibbling at it, you are passively losing wealth. It's like leaving a scale of candies out on the counter; its content slowly shrinks away.

Zooming out, the reason investing exists, or even why money exists, is because people have a need to store value. You earn something today and want to spend the fruits of your hard labor tomorrow. Or more realistic: you start working when you are young and want to make sure you save something to be able to maintain a comfortable way of living when you're old and retire. The *safest* investment, in that sense, would be to buy today the things you'll need at that time. For example, a house to live in is a near-perfect hedge for your future housing needs. But obviously, there are at least two issues with this strategy. One, you might not know what your cravings will be once you're in your seventies. And two, buying the eggs to consume them twenty years from now is obviously not the best smelling idea.

A friend of mine, let's call him Willy, once told me he wasn't interested in investing. Willy was often heard saying: "I'll keep my money in my checking account. It's safe there, so I don't need to worry about a thing." Willy also liked making fun of me every time newspapers headline that stocks are down. Fast forward two years: inflation at 6%, his checking account yields at 0.5%, and Willy is still sitting on the same pile of cash, slowly sinking into poverty. Like the Titanic, but without the dramatic music. The truth of the matter is, you're always betting on something. And the irony of the situation is that physical money and checking accounts, usually seen as the safest bet, are actually the riskiest if looked at over a longer time horizon: Willy is close to 100% sure of losing buying power over the next decade. Investment grade bonds yield slightly higher returns, but their fixed income nature make them equally risky: committing to receive a fixed return, while future inflation rates are a complete unknown, is a very hazardous bet to make. What should Willy do instead?

Arguably the best bet one can make is producing things the world needs today and for which chances are pretty high that future demand will still be there. When inflation spikes, selling prices for those products and services will rise too. As Warren Buffett would say: "For a young person, education and human capital is your best investment." Learn a skill for which there will be demand long in the future. It's your best bet to be able to earn a good living. The textbook example is the dentist; one can be pretty sure dentists will still be needed ten, twenty, or thirty years from now. Even AI and other innovations will probably not push them out of business for a very long time to come.

The investment equivalent of the dentist is to be the owner of a company that produces goods and services that will still be needed or wanted in the future. People liked to drink Coca-Cola fifty years ago, and they'll probably still like it fifty years down the road. Same with a Lotus Biscoff cookie. Or even clothes or luxury leather bags: Hermès was founded in 1837 and is still very much among us. So buying shares, and thus becoming co-owners, of such businesses is your safest bet if you're looking for a place to store your wealth.

Hourly wages versus Compounding returns

If you are still not convinced of the merits of investing, and letting your wealth compound, let the following example sink in.

Assume you developed an extremely valuable skill. People are willing to pay top dollars for your employment, so you can charge an hourly wage of a whopping

5,000 USD. Every hour, you earn 5,000 USD. Not only that, but you love your job, and found a way to stay awake at night and keep working: you do your job 24 hours a day, 365 days a year, nonstop earning 5,000 USD for every hour. Now assume you were born at the same time Jesus Christ was (allegedly) born, 2025 years ago, and managed to stay alive and keep working every single hour of every single day since then, charging 5,000 USD per hour over 2025 years. And not spending a dime during all that time. If you just kept your money in cash, without any compounding effects on your wealth, your net worth would total 88.7 billion USD[1]. Which is, at the time of writing, about one-third of the currently estimated net worth of Jeff Bezos. Or one-fifth of the net worth of Elon Musk. Or about half of the net worth of Warren Buffett.

Let that sink in. Wealth is not created by how many hours one works, or by what hourly rate you can charge. Wealth is created by letting your net worth compound at a faster rate than the world around you. At least equally important, this also works in reverse: poverty, or the loss of wealth, often doesn't come from one day to the next. More often, it erodes slowly, year-by-year, because of inflation exceeding the rate of return you realize on what you already have. Eating away your net worth. The cookie slowly crumbles away...

So if you don't find a way to make money while you sleep, you will work until you die.

Porsche-inflation

As an investor, there is a whole range of financial (stocks, bonds, ...) and not so financial products (wine, art, ...) you can choose from. History demonstrates that over the long run stocks—or rather, businesses—are the only viable investment choice to generate long-term investment returns above the inflation rate, and to maximize the compounding effect on your wealth. One of the reasons for this is that stocks are essentially return-generating assets of which—over the long run—the value should go up when inflation does. However, for most debt-related assets, this is not the case.

---

[1] 5,000 USD * 24 hours * 365,2425 days (including leap years and correcting for non-leap century years) * 2025 years = 88.753.927.500 USD to be exact.

One notable exception might be inflation-linked bonds. Unfortunately, even these are not as safe as the name suggests. Because while their coupon gets inflation-adjusted, the measure used for inflation is the CPI inflation, which is measured using the price changes of an average basket of consumer goods. But you are not an average person! So your average inflation differs from the one used by the government to calculate your next "inflation-adjusted coupon." Which implies that your hedge is not a hedge.

The thing is, most people aspire to become wealthier than the average person. (The people who have the money to invest, arguably already are.) But here comes the bad news: on average, aspirational consumption undergoes faster price hikes than the average consumer. You often hear the rich get richer, but goods the rich buy also get more expensive at a quicker rate. Poor guys!

> **"The rich getting richer" is a good thing.**
>
> Contrary to popular beliefs, "the rich getting richer", or "the gap between the rich and the poor is increasing" are actually positive evolutions. The reason why is linked to our freedom.
>
> In a free world, people can make choices, and those choices have an impact on their lives. But freedom also means some people—hopefully a minority—will consistently make the "wrong" choices and thus end up being poor. So the floor value is fixed: it means having nothing (but debt).
>
> So if the rich get richer, it means the "developed world" keeps developing, which is a good thing. It is also good because there are often spill-over effects to the entire community, benefiting everyone. So "the rich getting richer," or "the gap between the rich and the poor is increasing" are actually positive evolutions in the world.

To illustrate the point, below is the price chart of the manufacturer's suggested retail price of a world-famous sports car, the Porsche 911, over the time period 1964-2022. Over a 58-year period, prices for the 911-car increased to about fifteen times the initial value, from 6,490 USD to 101,200 USD. This implies an average price hike just shy of 5% per year. Over that same period of time, the CPI-index only increased by about eight times the initial amount, or 4% per year. Stated like that, the difference might sound small. But if you would have invested your 6,490 USD at a rate equalling the inflation-index, you would have had 61,235 USD in 2022. A cool 40k shy of what it actually took to be able to drive your 911 home from the dealership that year.

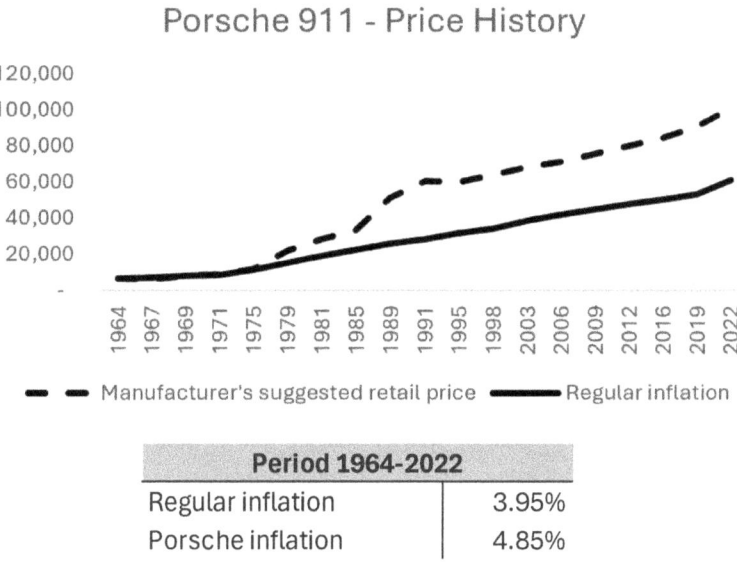

Period 1964-2022	
Regular inflation	3.95%
Porsche inflation	4.85%

I might hear you think: yes, but this comparison is not fair. A 911 in 1964 does not compare to the 2022 model. Technology advanced, and the current cars are way safer, have more horsepower, are connected to the internet, and are way more high-tech in general. While all this is true, it doesn't really matter: the old version was an advanced car at its time in 1964, and that's what the new one is today. To prove the point, this "Theorem of the Porsche-inflation," as one likes to call it, also applies to other luxury goods that are not prone to technological advancements. For example, a Louis Vuitton Speedy 25 bag. This luxury bag, originally commissioned by Audrey Hepburn in 1965, became part of the general sale shortly after. Today, it is still part of the Louis Vuitton catalogue, and is still desired by many high-heeled clients. One only found prices dating back to 1979, but that still gives us a forty-five year period to analyze. Over that time period, US CPI inflation averaged 3.22%. While the bag could be acquired for 150 USD in 1979, today it requires an outlay of 1,490 USD. For an average price hike of 5.36% per year over this entire period. So if you opted to invest your 1979 money in an asset that only tracked the CPI inflation, today you would be left *holding the bag*, but only in the shop. Because over this time period, your 150 USD would have grown to 605 USD, well short of the 2024 price tag of 1,490 USD.

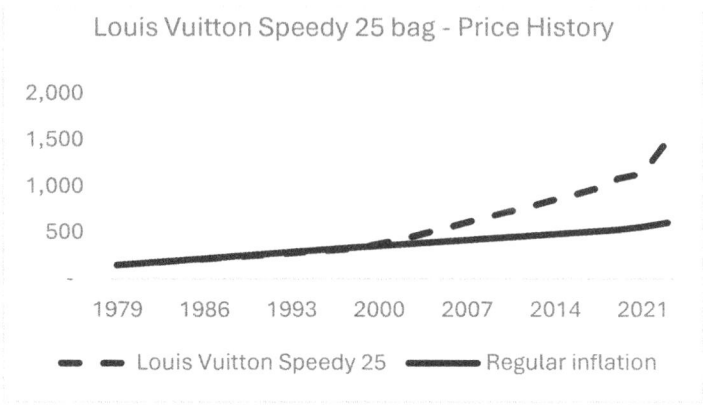

Period 1979-2023	
Regular inflation	3.22%
Louis Vuitton inflation	5.36%

Luxury goods appreciate quicker than other goods.

> **Theorem of the Porsche-inflation:**
>
> **The wealthier you are, the higher your personal inflation rate is.**

The reason for this might well be that the wealth of the richest people accumulates at a faster pace than the average. Let's imagine you are part of the 1,000 richest people in the world. If your wealth only accumulates at an average rate, then soon you will be overtaken by some people that are currently just below the top 1,000 who started making a better run than you did. And the top is the top. So to remain there, it's insufficient to have only average rates of return.

Also, to remain aspirational, the prices of goods that targets the high-end luxury segment needs to increase at an above-average speed as well, otherwise the goods become available to more potential customers, hence losing their exclusive or aspirational luster.

Luckily for aspirational investors, there are valuable lessons to be learned: it means over longer-term periods, the profitability of luxury brands keeps going up at the same rate as the Porsche-inflation, not the CPI inflation. And although this is implicitly assuming the luxury brands of today will manage to remain luxury brands tomorrow and for the long run, for most high-end brands this is the case. (This is both cause and effect for them to cherish their rich heritage. But more on brands, luxury goods, and stock picks later on in this book.)

The key takeaway so far is that, to increase your wealth, it is crucial to compound your net worth at a faster rate than the rest of the world around you. But the wealthier you (or your lifestyle) gets, the higher your personal inflation rate becomes.

Now, it is time to get a look at the long-term returns of the different investable asset classes, to see how this goal can or cannot be attained.

Returns of the different asset classes

In the previous section, it was briefly stated that bonds and fixed income, including the inflation-linked variants, barely enable its owner to preserve wealth. The facts for this statement are given below: the graph and table detail the long-term returns of equities, bonds, commodities, and gold.

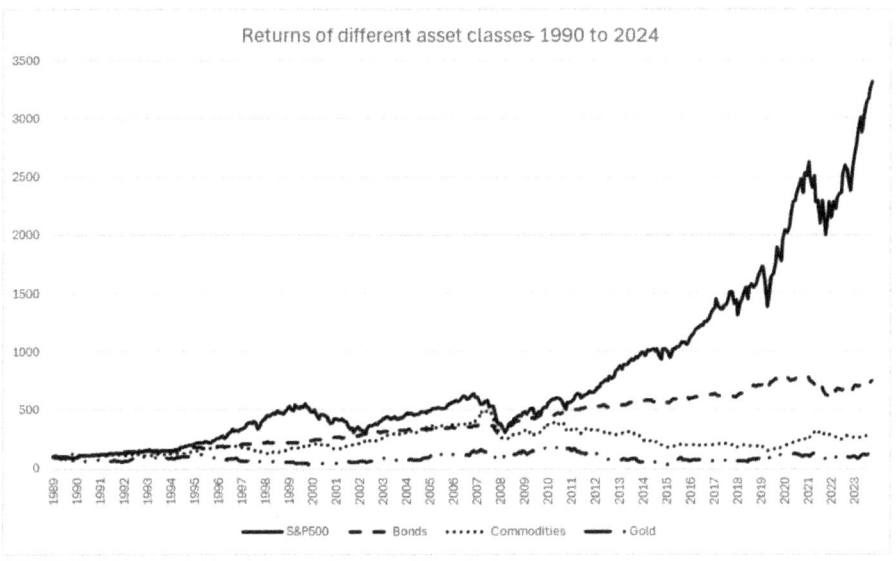

// WHY INVEST?

	S&P500	Bonds	Commodities	Gold
Return	10.61%	5.96%	2.99%	0.81%
Stdev	14.85%	5.87%	14.73%	35.97%

The returns speak for themselves: the historical returns on equities are way higher than any other credible investment alternative. And although there are small periods of time during which bonds or commodities outperform equities, these are often short-lived, and the timing of their occurrence is extremely hard to predict with an acceptable degree of accuracy. Therefore, one is better off staying invested in equities, instead of trying to predict the timing of the next market crash.

> ### Theorem of Time:
> **Time in the market is more important than timing the market**

The Investment Horizon trap

The sole exception, when equities are not the preferred choice to grow and protect your wealth, is perhaps if your investment horizon is short. This means that you expect large expenses during the next couple of months or years. E.g., If you plan on buying a house six months from now, it probably isn't the greatest plan to invest all your net worth in the stock market.

However, there are often misconceptions about the investment horizon. All too often it is stipulated that the investment horizon of a person in retirement is short by definition. And while this is true for some elderly people, it is not the case for others. If a market crash could have a severe impact on your standard of living, then indeed your investment horizon is shorter. Especially if your only means of living is your investment income. But lots of wealthy elderly people won't use up their net worth themselves and are basically investing to leave money for their kids or grandchildren, or for charity. All of these often do have a long investment horizon. Which implies that those elderly people also have a long investment horizon, often decades longer than even their own life expectancy: The investment horizon is determined by the goal of the individual.

But that leads us to **the core question of this book: which stocks should you buy? What companies are good to own, and at what price should you try to pick up the stock?** Or should you just buy an index fund?

Welcome to the world of stock picking! Time to get off the sidelines and get into the game. Your job as an investor isn't to avoid risk, but to manage it. This book should offer you the tools to help you do just that.

But before we start off, just one important disclaimer: There are a lot of different ways to look at the world. And there are a lot of different ways of investing. In this book, I merely describe my own views on investing: The best way is to find undervalued stocks and to let wealth compound, based on my own meandering experience. It is important to state that not everyone will agree with every single detail in this book. It is also not necessary to do so. In fact, I encourage readers to remain critical of every aspect of the investment process. Questioning everything and staying critical is—in my opinion—the correct mindset, and the single most important prerequisite to becoming a successful investor.

Chapter Summary

- Every asset is an investment. Including cash. So everyone has an (explicit or implicitly decided) asset allocation. Make your decisions consciously. Not deciding is actually also a de facto decision.
- The best way to increase your wealth is by compounding your net worth at a higher rate than the rest of the world.
- Theorem of the Porsche-Inflation: The wealthier your lifestyle, the higher your personal inflation becomes.
- The investor horizon is determined by the goal of the individual, which can be longer than the life expectancy of the person currently holding the stocks.

CHAPTER 2
Investment Philosophies

> *"The stock market is filled with individuals who know the price of everything, but the value of nothing."*
>
> – PHILIP FISHER

Now that we have established we want to buy stocks—ownership stakes in public companies—two new questions present themselves: which companies or businesses to buy, and at what price does their stock become attractive? This introduces us to the need for valuation techniques. Or does it?

Some theories suggest the price does not matter at all, and one should just buy all listed companies, regardless of price or activity. Others pursue the chase of buying stocks that became expensive just because they became expensive.

In this chapter, an overview of the most important—or most popular—investment techniques and philosophies will be given, together with the thought process behind it (if there is one). This overview does not pursue completeness, as that would encompass an entire book on its own.

Broadly speaking, investment theories can roughly be divided in following three streams:

- Value investing: determining the intrinsic value of a stock, and trying to find stocks that trade at a price significantly below this intrinsic value.
- Quality & Growth: buying companies that are growing and have a strong pricing power. Often these companies trade at higher price multiples than the market average, but their growth should make up for that.
- Momentum: buy rising stocks, regardless of their activity or valuation. If the stock recently became more popular and more expensive, chances are this trend will continue in the near future.

// INVESTMENT PHILOSOPHIES

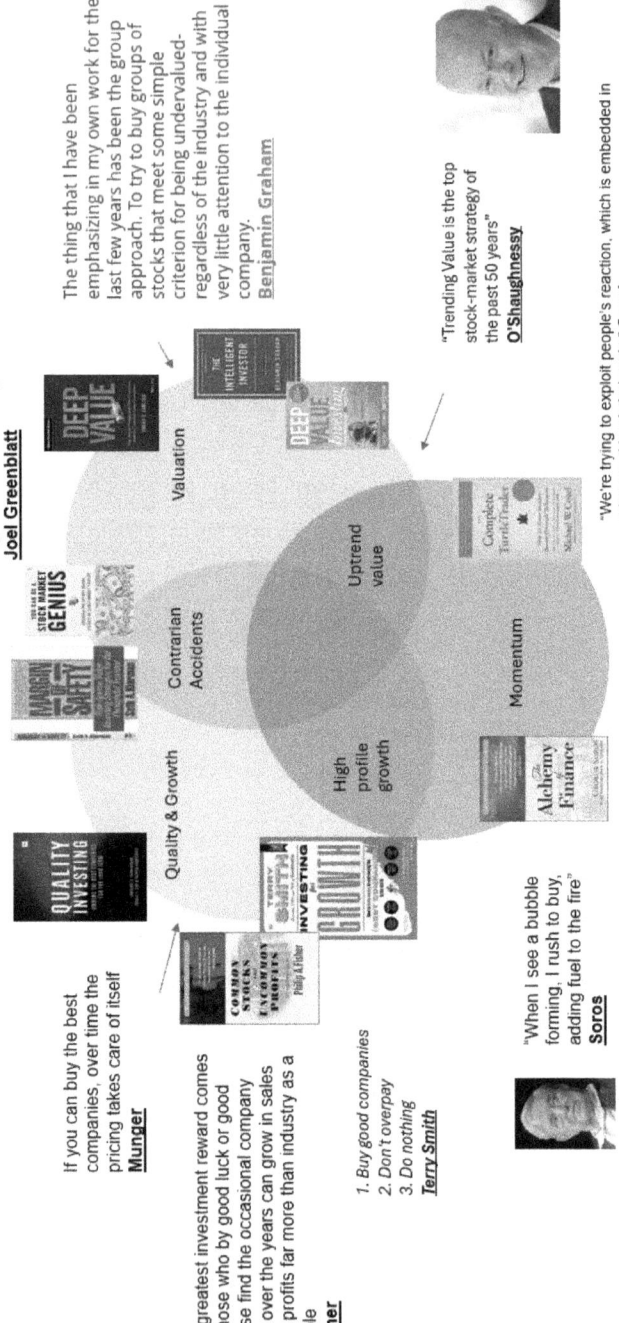

The thing that I have been emphasizing in my own work for the last few years has been the group approach. To try to buy groups of stocks that meet some simple criterion for being undervalued—regardless of the industry and with very little attention to the individual company.
Benjamin Graham

"Trending Value is the top stock-market strategy of the past 50 years"
O'Shaughnessy

"We're trying to exploit people's reaction, which is embedded in prices and leads to trends." **Covel**

A good business cheap
Joel Greenblatt

The prevailing view has been that the market will earn a high rate of return if the holding period is long enough, but entry point is what really matters.
Klarman

If you can buy the best companies, over time the pricing takes care of itself
Munger

the greatest investment reward comes to those who by good luck or good sense find the occasional company that over the years can grow in sales and profits far more than industry as a whole
Fisher

1. Buy good companies
2. Don't overpay
3. Do nothing
Terry Smith

"When I see a bubble forming, I rush to buy, adding fuel to the fire"
Soros

14

Value Investing

The classic way of investing, and of analyzing stocks, can loosely be seen as "value investing." It means one analyzes companies, tries to understand the business and its earnings model, and estimates what the intrinsic fair value is for the company. Then, this valuation is compared with the level where the stock is currently trading[2]. If the current market price is below the estimated intrinsic value, you buy the stock. And if its price moves above your estimated intrinsic value (or if your estimation changes and drops to a level below the current trading price) you sell the stock.

This should make intuitive sense, and is, loosely speaking, what happens with everything else one buys. E.g., if you want to buy a phone, you look around at all available phones, you know what functionalities you want, and if you find a model that you like, and if the price you can buy it at is below what it is worth to you, you buy the phone. The strange thing is that many people do more research when buying a 1,000 USD phone than they do when buying stocks for tenfold that amount or more.[3]

It is to be said that sometimes, value investing is misunderstood or seen as "buying cheap companies." "Cheap" is often defined as "companies with a low price/earnings ratio." This is not what is meant by "value investing" in this book. This is because, for one, the P/E ratio is not a good measure to use for valuing companies, as will be discussed later in this book, in Chapter 5. And two, a company might look cheap based on last year's earnings, but if the future prospects of the company are bleak, then actually that seemingly low price might still be overvalued compared to our estimate of the expected intrinsic value of the company. So, a "low price" alone is not sufficient. It needs to be low compared to what we estimate the company is truly worth.

---

[2] In this book, the terms "value of a company" and "stock value" are loosely used as synonymous. To clarify: The stock value times the number of stocks outstanding equals the "company value" or "market cap." Add the net debt, and you arrive at the "enterprise value."

[3] Don't blame them. The more uninformed investors there are in the market, the more mispricing opportunities will appear. And the better this is for investors who do their research thoroughly. Think about it as a game of poker: it pays off to play against *less sophisticated opponents*... (Note to self: maybe I should never publish this book?)

> **About risk, the stock price, and market movements**
>
> Except for the day you conduct a transaction, the stock price is irrelevant. It doesn't matter if your portfolio is up, down, moved sideways or in circles. If you are not going to buy or sell, the price someone is offering doesn't matter.
>
> An exception is if you bought with a lot of leverage, in which case a low price can cause margin calls. Those are to be avoided. And as you don't have any control over how Mr. Market will price your shares, my advice is to avoid leverage that is subject to margin calls, or at least keeping it at a very reasonable level. If you have 100 USD to invest, my advice is to not borrow more than 30 USD. It implies you end up with a portfolio of 130 USD invested, and 30 USD debt.
>
> The exact level depends on your risk appetite, the lending standards available to you, and your non-equity wealth (real estate, bonds and other assets). Also, there is absolutely nothing wrong with not borrowing at all.
>
> Always keep in mind that leverage works in two ways. And although stock markets generally go up over the long term—which implies that leverage will, on average, increase your wealth—a good night's sleep is also worth a lot. If you worry too much when stock markets go down, or when you're in debt, it's perfectly OK not to borrow.

Quality & Growth Investing

Few words in investing inspire more confidence than *quality* and *growth*. The idea is simple: buy a great company, and over time, its rising profits will justify the price you paid. This logic underpins the willingness of investors to pay ever-higher valuations for companies that are deemed "unstoppable," assuming that their dominance will continue indefinitely. After all, if a business keeps expanding, the stock price *has* to follow, right?

Warren Buffett famously remarked that "*it is better to buy a wonderful company at a fair price, than to buy a fair company at a wonderful price.*" There is undeniable wisdom in his words: a stock might appear expensive today, but if the company can double or triple its earnings in the coming years it could, in hindsight, turn out to be a bargain. So the art lies in finding *great companies*, that will indeed manage to keep growing and keep increasing their profits at a higher rate than everybody else. Hence the pursuit of finding companies with a "moat" around their business model: companies of which its products are highly desirable and cannot easily be copied or outcompeted by competitors or new market entrants.

While this investment philosophy holds plenty of truth—and some companies do grow into their lofty valuations—many investors conveniently forget that even the best businesses can falter. Competition intensifies, industries shift, and what once seemed like an unshakable empire can lose its edge. (Anyone remember Nokia? Blackberry? IBM? Intel?) The risk isn't just that growth slows. It's that expectations were so high to begin with that even a minor disappointment can send prices tumbling.

In reality, no stock is immune to gravity. Growth is essential, but assuming it will always "take care of the price" can be a costly mistake. Even the best companies are still just investments, and no investment is worth an infinite price. Looking for a combination of "great companies" which grow profitably, that at the same time trade at a "fair to cheap price" should be the bread-and-butter play of the intelligent investor. But great companies rarely come cheap. The art of investing lies in striking the right trade-off: paying *a little more* for a significantly higher-quality business that justifies the premium.

The real skill isn't just in identifying *great companies*, but in knowing when the price is right.

Momentum Investing

A completely different investment philosophy is found in momentum investing.

Increasing prices and success stories attract attention and money. As prices climb and success stories flood the headlines, the lure of quick wealth becomes irresistible to many. Whether it's stocks, commodities like gold and coffee, or the latest cryptocurrency, rising prices fuel a frenzy of interest, drawing in more and more investors. Herding behavior takes hold. Driven by the fear of missing out, people rush to invest, believing they can ride the wave to riches. After all, what could be worse than watching a neighbor strike it big while you sit on the sidelines? Yet, this kind of speculative investing is more akin to gambling than investing. While a lucky few may master the art of timing the market – or just be on a lucky strike – and walk away with a fortune, the vast majority find themselves caught in a bubble destined to burst, leaving them with little more than regret and empty pockets.

Meme-Stock Investing

Meme-stock investing is one example of this behavior. It refers to the practice of buying and selling stocks based on their popularity on social media platforms and online forums, rather than making investments based on company fundamentals or traditional financial metrics. It's like betting on a horse race where everyone is cheering for the same horse. Not because it's the fastest, but because it's the most exciting one. In the long run, fundamentals will catch up, and the excitement will fade. Which leaves speculative investors very vulnerable. The entire investment strategy is built on "finding a greater fool" which offers more money for the same piece of paper.

If you are able to sell in time (and avoid being the last one to hold on to the paper when the music stops), this strategy can be extremely rewarding. Keith Gill, using the aliases *Roaring Kitty* and *DeepFuckingValue* (pardon my French) is the most notable speculator who is seemingly successfully applying this strategy.

In a way, momentum investing is also one of the strategies applied by George Soros. Although not based on forums and social media posts, his theory of reflexivity basically states that markets are not driven by fundamentals alone. Biases of market participants impact prices, and might result in a positive feedback loop: buyers increase prices and (paper) profits, which attracts more buyers, which builds the bubble. And in Soros's words: "*When I see a bubble forming, I rush in to buy, adding fuel to the fire.*" Indeed, bubbles can be extremely rewarding, on the condition that you step on the train early enough, and that you jump off before the train wrecks...

An exchange of ideas, or market manipulation?

It helps if one masters the skill of creating a hype himself. By writing about a stock, some people manage to get others to act and buy or sell, which moves the stocks in the desired direction. Often, the lines of legality get blurred: what is the difference between "an honest exchange of ideas" and "trying to pump up the stock, then sell at a large profit"? And what is "freedom of speech" versus "market manipulation"? The sensibilities of this discussion are beyond the scope of this book, but nonetheless this is a very interesting topic.

Other Investment Philosophies

Lots of different people have lots of different opinions. That's what keeps the world moving and the stock market fluctuating. Always remember: For every trade[4] there is someone on the other side of the trade. For every stock you buy, there is someone happy to sell at the exact same price. So trading is some sort of zero-sum game. (Investing is not, luckily. Because companies on average make a profit, so in the end, on average *everyone is a winner.*")

In what follows, a non-exhaustive list of other investment philosophies is described. Of which some of them were also successfully applied by a number of great investors.

Index Investing & the efficient market hypothesis

The most popular investment method at the moment is not value investing, but index investing. This theory basically states that all available public information is immediately incorporated in the stock price. Which implies that the price of a stock is always correct. So trying to find undervalued stocks is a useless waste of time, according to this theory. The concepts—and fallacies—of this thought process will be discussed more at length in Chapter 3.

---

[4] With the sole exception perhaps of an IPO or capital increase, in which a company creates new stocks to raise capital for working needs or to finance expansion plans.

// INVESTMENT PHILOSOPHIES

Factor Investing and Quant Investing

As time went on, more research was performed. It was observed that some simple rules of thumb lead to higher returns over the long run. The most well-known[5] are:

- Small companies provide better stock returns than large companies
- Cheap companies (low price-to-book ratio) perform better than expensive companies
- Momentum: Stocks that have been rising in price often keep rising, while stocks that have lost value often keep losing.

Before you knew it, there were more factors than stocks, which is just one of the reasons to prove that markets are not efficient at all. By choosing the right stocks, you can outperform the market. In order to defend the original theory, some academics desperately tried to come up with reasons to explain why some factors are outperforming. For example, by saying that investing in smaller companies is riskier compared to investing in larger companies. However, it is hard to explain why cheaper stocks would be riskier compared to expensive stocks. Same thing for momentum, and for all the other factors.

Our favorite factor? Companies that had SEC members visiting their headquarters on average underperform the markets in the months after these visits, compared to companies that did not have an SEC visit. This strategy sounds difficult to apply in real life, as the SEC is not publishing a list of companies being visited by their employees. However, telecom companies and app developers collect data of mobile phone locations. If a phone is in an SEC building during office hours more often than not, one can assume this phone belongs to an SEC employee. And if that employee visits the head office of a listed company during business hours, this ... tells you something about the average future stock performance of that company. As it increases the chance that the company conducting fraudulent behavior, and/or will receive a fine.[6] This shows that thorough research, in even the most far-sought strategies, can pay off.

---

[5] First published in the Three-Factor Model Paper (1993). Fama, Eugene F. and Kenneth R. French (1993). "Common Risk Factors in the Returns on Stocks and Bonds." Journal of Financial Economics 33(1): 3–56.

[6] As documented in the paper "Watching the Watchdogs: Tracking SEC Inquiries using Geolocation Data" (2024), by William Christopher Gerken, Steven Irlbeck, Marcus Painter, Guangli Zhang.

Something about crypto

These days one can't write a book about investing without spending a word or two about crypto. But in order to state the obvious, let's take a step back and look at what an investment in equity really is, and then compare it to crypto and private equity.

In **listed equity**, the owner of a stock is a part-owner of a business. And next to that business, there is a line that depicts the *perceived* value of that business: the market price. Which may or may not be a fair representation of the real intrinsic value of the business.

The disadvantage of having this line is that it can distract the attention. Instead of watching the company, people start looking at that line: the stock price. Because that one moves a lot, is volatile, and moves every moment of the day, people can talk and write about it. However, the company itself is more boring, predictable, and often a different picture with new information is available only every quarter, instead of every millisecond.

Human eyes and attention are attracted to movement. Next time you walk in a park, just try to stare, and try not to focus on that dog running around. Doing so is harder than you think!

There are only two problems with this. One, it's an enormous waste of time and energy to constantly watch that line. And two, management might start trying to manage that line, rather than managing the company. They might feel the urgency to take actions whenever the line moves. This overreaction can cause value destructive decisions.

Private equity offers a solution to the volatility and speculation of public markets by removing the constant price fluctuations. When a company is taken private—or remains private—there are no daily stock transactions, meaning there's no constantly shifting market value to influence investor sentiment. Without this ever-present "line" tracking short-term price movements, ownership of the company only changes hands based on carefully negotiated agreements rather than impulsive market reactions. This stability comes at a cost: investors lose the ability to buy or sell shares instantly. Yet, this lack of liquidity should encourage a more strategic, long-term approach, shielding investors from the noise and emotional swings of public markets.[7]

Crypto on the other hand, is the complete opposite. Instead of getting rid of the line, someone somewhere thought: why not just get rid of the company? Let's just keep the line—keep trading a token—without having a company underneath. Who needs the underlying cashflow generating company, if you can just trade hot air?

In a sense, this was a genius move. History is full of scams in which people try to cook the accounting books or run Ponzi schemes. But this is hard work, and tough to do: you need a registered company, fill out paperwork, keep a store front, and keep up appearances. It is way easier to just get rid of it all, and trade hot air instead! All you need is a bunch of servers making needless calculations to solve puzzles (let's call them *hashes*) to heat up the air, and you're all set…

Previous versions of this were "virtual real estate" in games, and later Non-Fungible Tokens (NFTs) appeared. The arguments of *digital scarcity* and *owning a piece of the metaverse* were used to make speculative investments sound like visionary opportunities rather than what they really were: high-risk gambles. Some people managed to make millions. A lot of others were left empty-pocketed after the bubble burst.

So if your goal is to try to get rich quickly, try crypto. Or a roulette wheel, for that matter. Go to the casino and try your luck. You might even get free drinks while doing so. In this book, however, the focus is on investing in real companies with real cashflows. Which gives a much larger success rate of actually generating value and becoming wealthier. But it is also almost a guarantee that wealth creation will go more slowly.

In the stock market, patience is a virtue. Especially when compounding is at your side…

---

[7] It also saves the need for a bunch of reporting requirements.

Practice what you preach

A final remarkable observation we'd like to make is that investing is probably one of the very few fields that are often taught by people with very little field experience. Many finance professors have literally never owned a stock, let alone worked at an investment company, run a mutual fund or worked at a hedge fund. Yet nobody seems to question this. Imagine being a surgical student and being taught by people who have never spent any part of their career near an operating room. In finance and investing, these days this all seems normal.

Chapter Summary

- The classic investment approach is value investing. This still makes a lot of sense and can be described as "buying stocks if the price is below your estimation of its intrinsic value".

- Value investing is often misunderstood as "buying companies that have a low price/earnings ratio." However, this is not value investing: companies can be cheap for good reasons (bleak outlook for the company).

- Quality investing states that if you buy a great company, the price will take care of itself. While this philosophy offers valuable insights, blindly buying great companies at any price can lead to disaster. However, blending these principles with the fundamentals of value investing creates a compelling and balanced approach. The art is in finding the sweet spot of 'quality at an affordable price'.

- Momentum investing implies "buying what went up in value." Some people do this successfully. Our advice? Don't try this at home.

- Next to value investing and momentum investing, there are tons of other methodologies to invest your money on the stock market: index investing and factor investing, just to name a few examples.

- Do not invest your life savings in the latest hype, like crypto. Remember metaverse real estate? Remember NFTs?

CHAPTER 3

The Non-Efficient Market Hypothesis

"In stock market, the price is always wrong."

JENS VERBRUGGE

In academic literature, the concept of "the efficient market hypothesis" (EMH) is still taught as a core concept and as a factual truth. This theory is credited to Eugene Fama, in his 1970s paper "Efficient Capital Markets: a Review of Theory and Empirical Work." The theory, evolved over the years, can exist in three primary forms, often referred to as weak, semi-strong, and strong forms of efficient markets.

In **weak-form efficient markets**, the theory suggests that current asset prices reflect all past market data, such as historical prices, trading volumes, and patterns. It implies that technical analysis—predicting future stock prices using past price data—will not lead to abnormal returns. Because all that data is already "priced in." But fundamental stock analysis—based on analyzing the economy, the financials of the company, and its competitive position—might still lead to such above-average returns.

In **semi-strong efficient markets**, it is assumed that current market prices do reflect all publicly available information. This means no abnormal returns can be obtained, even when analyzing all publicly available information about the company, its competitors, the economy, et cetera. This implies that neither technical analysis nor fundamental analysis can lead to abnormal stock returns.

Some people even take it one step further: in **strong-form efficient markets**, it is assumed that all information, including public, private, and insider information, gets priced in. Even insider buying (an illegal activity in almost all jurisdictions!) cannot lead to abnormal stock returns.

In reality, though, large price fluctuations of individual stocks can often be observed, which cannot be attributed to any news flow. Furthermore, stock prices often exhibit positive momentum: a stock that went up recently, has a higher probability to keep going up in the near future, which implies that markets are not efficient, even in its weakest form.

This, too, is recognized in other parts of the academic literature. For example, that very same Eugene Fama developed a three-factor model together with Kenneth French in 1992. In which it is shown that stocks of smaller companies, with cheaper price-book ratios, outperform the markets in general over longer periods of time. And this effect cannot be attributed to an increase in the risk level taken.

In 2015, this model was further enhanced, and Fama and French published their five-factor model that adds that companies with a higher profitability, and with a more conservative investment policy, outperform the market on a risk-adjusted basis.

Also, Joel Greenblatt's "Magic Formula" that recommends buying stocks with low historical EV/EBIT ratios and high Returns on Capital (ROC), outperforms the markets. And the formula keeps working over extended periods of time, which would be impossible according to the Efficient Market Hypothesis.

During that same period, Tversky and Kahneman published academic papers also showing that investment decisions are not as rational as efficient market theories expect. Human beings are not always 100% rational, and there is no proof that this would be any different when it comes to making investment decisions. On the contrary, all too often people react extremely emotionally to topics involving money.

To give an extreme example, money is one of the most common motives for murder, second only to love or revenge. Both of these are rarely driven by rational decision-making.

Therefore, and by observing the markets over a couple of decades, I developed my own hypothesis regarding stock prices:

> ## The Theorem of Verbrugge:
> ## "The Stock Price is Always Wrong."

The basis of this theorem is based on three obvious observations. One, that nobody knows the true value of a stock. Predicting the future is difficult, and thus so is predicting the future profitability of companies. However, some people are better at making predictions about certain stocks that others. But the best investors do not necessarily manage the largest pot of money, and thus do not cause the price of the stock to move towards that "best estimate" valuation figure.

Over time, strong investment returns naturally attract more capital. As a result, top-performing investment managers tend to oversee increasingly larger sums. However, people evolve over the years. With greater experience and wealth, their interests and incentives may shift, potentially leading to a decline in performance. This often results in once-exceptional money managers delivering less impressive returns, while latecomers to their investment funds grumblingly have to settle for subpar outcomes. The same principle applies in other fields—after all, the world's best chess players from twenty years ago are no longer winning championships today.

Two, and as seen earlier, behavioral biases and emotions might also play a role. There are also studies showing that hedge fund managers underperform the markets by 4.33% on average in the six-month period surrounding a divorce[8]. Personal events, behavioral biases, and pressure may affect the decision-making process of every retail and every professional investor.

And three, and maybe the most obvious one of them all, is that many retail investors are not really spending a whole lot of time or effort doing the work and performing the research. The phenomenon of meme-stock investing, as discussed in the previous chapter, serves as an extreme example. Many people spend more time researching the purchase of their next washing machine than they do buying stock.

But also in index investing, the price of a stock is irrelevant. Or even worse: the more overvalued a stock gets, the more weight it gets assigned in market-cap

---

[8] See paper "Limited attention, marital events and hedge funds", 1996, by Lu Yan, Sugata Ray and Teo Melvyn.

weighted indices. At the same time, nobody is held accountable for the final asset allocation: the index providers "just give a formula to show what the markets performed as a whole." And the (passive) fund managers almost blindly mimic the index composition so that their portfolio performance closely tracks the index performance. Because their task is to "just try to track the performance of the index as close as possible," without investigating the valuation of the index as a whole, let alone to evaluate the value of each constituent of the index individually.

A more philosophical way to describe why the stock price is always wrong is that there is not a clear-cut way to state what a company is worth. It all depends on the future. Although later chapters in this book will give guidelines and handles for evaluating a company relative to the value of other companies and assets, don't expect one single formula that gives an exact valuation to a stock. It is impossible to know the correct value with 100% certainty, without the knowledge of many years into the future[9].

Below are a number of stock price evolutions.

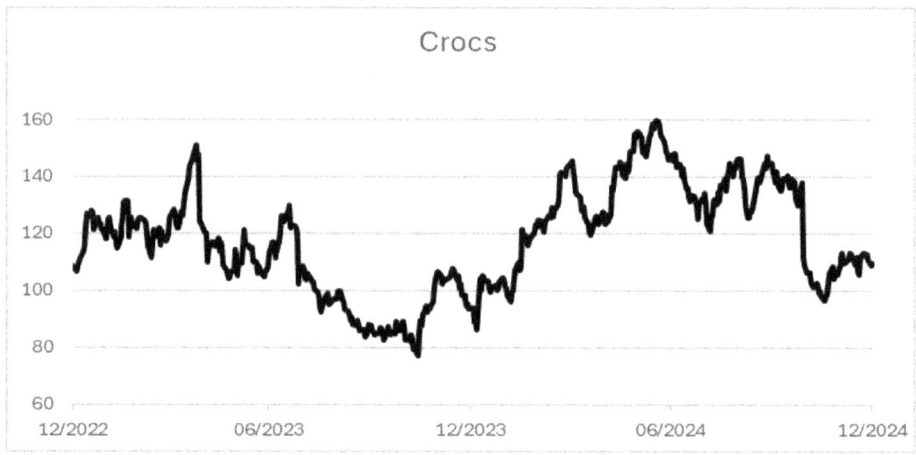

---

[9] One can even take it another step further: something can be worth more to you than it is to me. So the very existence of one single "correct" price might even be thrown into question...

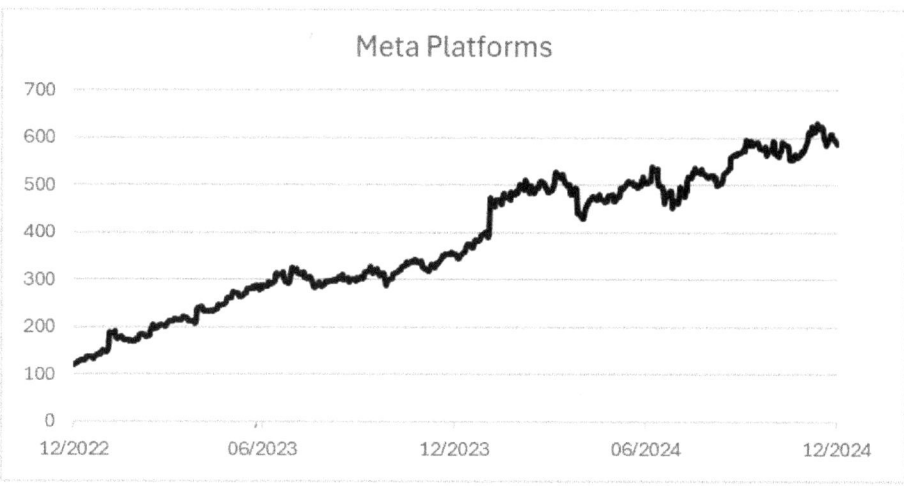

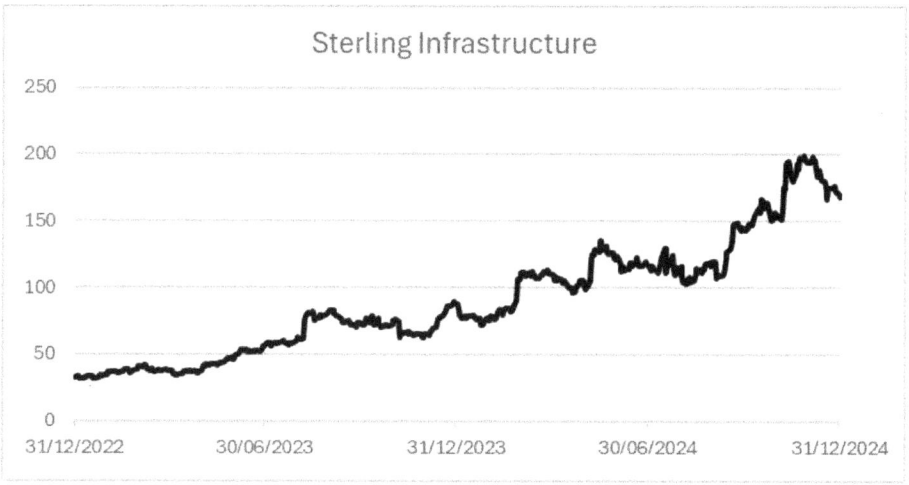

Ask yourself:

- Did the true value of a (visually unattractive) plastic shoe producer really fluctuate up and down by a factor of two multiple times over the last few years?
- Was Facebook, Instagram and WhatsApp owner Meta Platforms really worth six times more at the end of 2024, compared to two years prior to that?
- The same question can be asked for Sterling Infrastructure.

// THE NON-EFFICIENT MARKET HYPOTHESIS

Did these companies truly fluctuate so much in value? Or was the stock price often (or always) wrong?

The (Un)Usability of the Discounted Cash Flow Model

Nonetheless, just about every book on valuation explains the discounted Cash Flow model ("DCF model"). And it needs to be said, the core concept and the academic idea behind the model are very sound and very correct: the present value of an investment is worth the sum of its future cashflows, discounted to today.

Assume a very simplified example in which an asset is generating a 100 USD return every year. This income stream does not increase or decrease on economic conditions or inflation and does not need any additional investment requirements to keep generating this return. Then the value of this income stream can be calculated by:

$$Present\ value\ of\ FCF = \frac{yearly\ FCF}{r}$$

The discount rate "r" reflects the opportunity costs and risk associated with the investment. It equals the "risk-free rate"—the rate received on US government bonds, for companies doing business in USD—plus a risk premium to reflect the uncertainty of the income stream compared to these government bonds.

For example, for a perpetual bond, the FCF is the yearly coupon, and this formula gives a useful handhold to come up with a fair value of this stream of incomes.

If the bond is not a perpetual bond, but has a maturity date, the calculation becomes:

$$\begin{aligned}Present\ &value\ of\ FCF \\ &= \frac{coupon\ in\ year\ 1}{(1+r)^1} + \frac{coupon\ in\ year\ 2}{(1+r)^2} + \cdots \\ &+ \frac{coupon\ in\ year\ n}{(1+r)^n} + \frac{Face\ Value\ of\ the\ bond}{(1+r)^n}\end{aligned}$$

As a thought experiment, one can think of a stock in a similar fashion: the security might pay out a yearly or quarterly dividend, and the company might be sold or liquidated in the somewhat distant future. In the formula above, the fixed coupon is then to be replaced by the estimated dividend, and the "Face Value of the bond" becomes the Terminal Value of the company.

Assuming a fixed growth rate, this terminal value can be calculated as:

$$Terminal\ Value = \frac{FCF\ in\ the\ final\ year * (1 + g)}{r - g}$$

In which the FCF is the cash generated by the company, after all costs to run the business, and after all investments required to generate the assumed growth rate g.

Although this model is theoretically correct and can be a valuable way to think about the investment process, there are a couple of problems with the practical application of this approach. The first one being that the model is very sensitive to its input values. Let's illustrate this with a hands-on example. Assume a security that provides a 10 USD dividend per year, that increases by 5% in perpetuity. Assume a discount rate of 8%. This income stream is worth a present value of 10*(1.05)/(0.08-0.05) = 350 USD. Now if, for whatever reason, the growth rate drops half a percent to 4.5% and the discount rate increases half a percent to 8.5%, then the security value drops to 261.25 USD. A staggering 25% drop in value, considering the limited changes in the assumptions made.

If we then look at how good analysts are at estimating future earnings of companies, we get a sobering view. Let's take a look at Novo Nordisk, a Danish pharmaceutical company with a market cap of over 300 billion USD. The company is followed by a wide range of financial analysts all over the world. Yet when asking industry professionals to estimate the Earnings Per Share (EPS) for this company, answers vary wildly. They also change significantly over time.

The graph below pictures the so-called "consensus estimate" or the average estimation of the expected EPS that Novo Nordisk will post over book years 2024 and 2025. At the end of 2021, it was thought that the company would earn 14.3 DKK/share in 2024, and 16.0 DKK/share in 2025. Fast-forward, and three years later the average estimation increased to almost 23 USD/share for the (finished but not yet reported on) numbers of 2024, and 28.4 USD/share for the year 2025. Similarly large estimation errors can be observed for other companies.

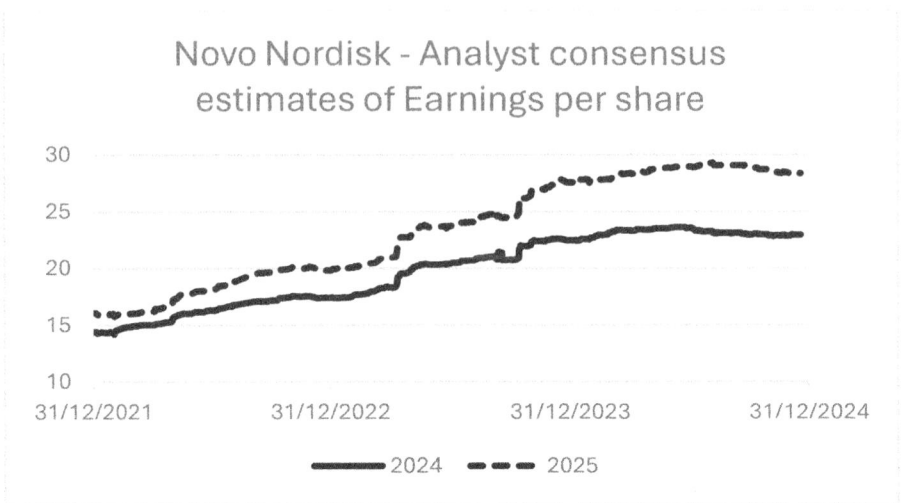

Needless to say, if the estimation error is over 60% (23 DKK/share versus 14.3 DKK/share) for earnings only three years forward, that the estimation of the "intrinsic value" for Novo Nordisk using the DCF-model—which is very sensible to input changes, and requires estimates until eternity—will vary so extremely that it becomes essentially worthless.

And this is for a company followed by many analysts, for earnings in the not-so-distant future. Then how useful is this model for small and midcap companies, followed by one or two analysts at most? Or for commodities players, subject to large swings in commodity prices?

In short, the DCF model is theoretically correct, but the practical usability to determine fair stock prices is limited to applications where the cashflows are very predictable. Two examples where it can be useful:

> ▸ A first example is a Real Estate Investment Trust (REIT) that owns a set of buildings that are rented out on long-term contracts with predictable pricing formulas to creditworthy tenants. And for which the REIT itself is financed by long-term debt at predictable interest rates. In such a case both the cash inflows and outflows are predictable for periods long into

the future. So the DCF-model can be somewhat useful. (One can still discuss the required discount rates to divide by.)

- A second example is not at a company level, but at a project level. E.g. a manager having to decide whether to let tasks do by manual labor, or by buying a machine and partially automating the process. It is often known what the machine costs and what the cost of labor is. If accurate predictions are available on what the maintenance costs, utilization rate and useful lifetime of the machine is, then a DCF model can be made for both the "manual labor" and the "buy the machine" options, and those two can be compared to determine the preferred option.

The key takeaway from this chapter is that the stock price is always wrong. And that the correct value today is also not calculatable with a high degree of certainty. Only rough estimations can be made, and even the savviest of analysts will often be wrong.

Does it make sense to buy stocks if their trade price is always wrong?

With this wisdom in mind, one might question whether estimating the intrinsic value of a stock is even a worthwhile endeavor. After all, even if a stock is deemed undervalued, there is no guarantee it will ever trade at its so-called "fair value." If an investor purchases a stock at a bargain price but never finds a buyer willing to pay what it is truly worth, does the initial discount hold any real significance? In such a case, is it even worth it to invest in the stock at all?

Assume you are at an auction and have the option to bid on a suitcase of which it is known that there is one million dollars in cash in the suitcase. However, the case is closed, locked, and there is no way for you to open the suitcase without damaging the content, being the Franklin bills. What is a fair price for the suitcase, or what should a "rational" investor bid for this? Answers can vary from zero to one million dollars, and there is not an objective way to say what the true value is...

// THE NON-EFFICIENT MARKET HYPOTHESIS

Does this mean that the same applies for stocks? The money is locked up in a company, and as a minority shareholder you have no real power to "open the suitcase"?

No. It does make sense to analyze companies, and value stocks[10]. To illustrate why this situation differs, consider a hypothetical company, CheapChimp Inc, with an intrinsic value of $100 per share, annual earnings of $10 per share, and a market price of $50, or half of its intrinsic value. Meanwhile, its competitor, OverpriceBull Inc, has the same intrinsic value and earnings per share but trades at $200, or twice its intrinsic worth.

If both companies distribute their earnings as dividends[11], CheapChimp's shareholders receive a generous 20% dividend yield ($10 on a $50 investment), whereas investors in OverpriceBull collect a mere 5% yield ($10 on a $200 investment). Even if stock prices remain unchanged over time, long-term investors in CheapChimp fare better simply due to the higher return on their initial investment—assuming, of course, that profits are indeed distributed via dividends.

However, if the companies choose to allocate their earnings toward share buybacks instead of dividends, the advantage for CheapChimp becomes even more pronounced. Over the course of five years, CheapChimp would generate $50 in earnings per share—enough to repurchase all outstanding shares. As a result, an investor who held onto their stake from the beginning would become the sole shareholder, effectively owning the entire company outright. This would grant them full control, including the ability to replace the board, appoint themselves CEO, and claim the company's full intrinsic value.

By contrast, OverpriceBull, despite generating the same per-share earnings, would only be able to repurchase one-quarter of its shares in the same timeframe. It would take significantly longer for an investor to reach a position of total ownership and unlock the company's full value, or be able to "open the suitcase". Thus, once again, CheapChimp proves to be the superior investment choice.

---

[10] Phew, otherwise this book would be very short, and your expense on the purchase of it would have been such a waste!

[11] And assuming there is no tax.

Admittedly, this is a theoretical example. However, if this scenario does not play out as described, it implies that the stock must appreciate in value—because if it doesn't, this outcome inevitably becomes reality.

In real life, there is often an implicit floor on how much a company can be undervalued. If the price becomes too ridiculously low, either the management of the company itself, or a private equity fund (or a combination of both) will attempt an acquisition and delist the company.

However, there is no such thing on the other side: there is no implicit ceiling. A company that is overvalued can remain overvalued for extended periods of time and even become more ridiculously overpriced. As famous hedge fund manager David Einhorn states it, *"Twice a ridiculous price is not twice as ridiculous"*. And yes, short selling—lending and selling a stock in an attempt to buy it back at lower prices at a later point in time—is in theory something that should limit the overvaluation of a stock. But in practice, because of the asymmetric payoff[12], government regulation[13] and the unpopularity of short sellers in general[14], the downward pressure for hyped stocks is very limited. Which means companies from Tesla to Virgin Galactic can remain vastly overvalued for extended periods of time.

This also implies that one of the most difficult aspects of investing is in fact knowing when to SELL a share. Lots of literature describes on when to buy a stock. But when to sell? If you sell as soon as (your estimate of) the intrinsic value is reached, you can miss out on a lot of upsides. Because momentum and FOMO might lead to large stock price increases, far beyond the fair value of the stock. At the same time, it is irrational to hold on to a stock if its price is higher than your estimate of its intrinsic value. Or to hold on to a stock that you would not buy anymore at the current price, which is a behavioral bias itself. A separate chapter of this book is dedicated to helping you decide when to sell a stock, including

---

[12] Short sellers have a limited upside potential and an unlimited downside risk.

[13] For example, UCITS-funds sold to retail investors in Europe are not allowed to take short-positions.

[14] People who profit from the misfortunes or downfall of a company are not very popular. They make their money at a time when the company needs to announce losses, layoffs, or declare bankruptcy. So it appears as if they profit from the misfortune of others. And the financial education of the general public is too limited to understand that they actually do have a useful role in making financial markets somewhat more efficient, thus providing companies with a more correct cost-of-capital.

guidelines and a discussion on traps to avoid. (It's called "Chapter 11" in this book but, spoiler alert, you shouldn't wait till a company files for chapter 11 before selling your stocks!!!)

Chapter Summary

- In academic literature, one can find all sorts of theories. Ranging from "markets are always 100% efficient" to "all investors have behavioral biases".
- My theory: The stock price is always wrong.
- Forget about DCF-models for valuing stocks. Although theoretically correct, in most practical cases the outcome of the model is too sensitive on the exact values of estimated inputs.
- Making exact calculations of the true value of a stock is impossible, because one cannot perfectly predict the future. But making an estimation of the intrinsic value of a stock is still a very valuable and financially rewarding exercise.
    - Buy if the stock is (far) below your estimation of its intrinsic value.
    - Selling is a more difficult exercise that will be discussed in a later chapter (11).

CHAPTER 4
The Perfect Company

"Hannah Montana said nobody's perfect, but here I am."

– Daniel Ricciardo

In chapter 2, during a discussion about the different investment philosophies, it was argued that investing in quality companies at a reasonable price can offer the best investment returns. In chapter 3, it was stated that the price at which stocks trade fluctuates wildly. And that the academically popular DCF-method is not practically useful for the hands-on investor. Before diving deeper into different valuation techniques—to determine what a "cheap" or reasonable price is for a company—let's first determine what types of companies one wants to buy. What are the qualities and characteristics to look for to find great companies?

In this chapter, those characteristics will be described. However, the perfect company is a bit like the perfect partner: it does not exist. Compromises will have to be made.

A Good Business

The perfect company is a high-quality business. It has a **moat** around its business model: your product or service cannot easily be replicated. There are different possible reasons why a company can have a moat.

Companies can have a **technological advantage**. For example, chips producer Nvidia is currently ahead of competition in the development of chips for AI-driven computing. And ASML produces photolithography machines used in the production of chips that are so advanced that currently nobody else manages to copy their products or is able to compete with them. If you are technologically ahead, you can charge a premium compared to what competitors are charging for their inferior products. At least, as long as you can remain ahead of the competition. This is the only downside to this type of moat: you need to keep investing in R&D, and keep improving your products, otherwise sooner or later competition will catch up.

Another source for having a moat can be **brand recognition**. If you own a very well-known brand that is associated with good quality products, consumers will prefer your product over the one of your competitors. Therefore, you can charge a premium and realize higher margins than your lesser-known competitors can. A moat like this can be built in different ways. The obvious one is to spend a lot of money on marketing. However, those dollars need to be spent wisely: if the additional marketing expenses are higher than what you will be able to surcharge your customers for the brand recognition, the marketing expense is just burning money.

Other ways of building brand recognition can be to perform stunts that get free media attention. Richard Branson's Virgin was a master in this, catching worldwide attention by attempting to be the first one to fly around the world in a hot air balloon in the end of the 1990s, or more recently by having the first commercial space flight in 2021. Red Bull is another notable example, focusing on anything from Formula One racing to Extreme Sports events.

A third way to build branding power is linked to our first type of moat, the technological advantage one: being an early mover to come up with a certain product. Kleenex is so well known that the product name became almost a synonym for disposable facial tissue. Googling became a verb. WD-40 is another example. And dating app Tinder became so well known it is the first app people think about when talking about dating. Notice that in most cases, they were not the first mover. But they became the first product that gained widespread popularity. A combination of technological innovations and good marketing can do wonders when an industry is being (re)invented. The fruits of it are often reaped for many decades in the future if you can get yourself in such a position.

A third way to get a moat is by having it **granted by the government**. A **patent** hindering competitors to attack your business is a very powerful tool in the pharmaceutical sector: generic copies of your medicine are only allowed after expiration of the patent (which usually lasts for 15 or 20 years). Also here, a link with innovation is at least useful, and in most cases a necessary requirement for obtaining such a moat.

Other ways to have regulatory grants are to have certain **licenses**. For example, in most jurisdictions it is not that easy to start up a bank or insurer from scratch. Telecom operators have their spectrum space licenses, as do radio operators. A potential drawback is that those licenses often come with a cost: in banking, it means having to adhere to strict regulations and heavy reporting requirements. In telecom, spectrum space is granted based on auctions, for which big bucks are to be paid.

Another way to have a moat is to have **network effects**: having more users increases the value proposition of your product for every additional user. This can work in different ways:

- Social media networks are more interesting if all your friends and connections are already using it. Twitter, Instagram or even WhatsApp or Tinder are not that difficult a product to copy from a software-point-of-view. But a competitor providing a similar, or even slightly superior product, will have difficulties becoming successful. Nobody will start using it, because nobody is using it.
- A different type of network effect is user knowledge. Think AutoCAD in the engineering world, Bloomberg terminals in the financial world, or Microsoft Excel just about everywhere: All companies use it, because all employees already know how to use it. Whereas switching to a different provider of similar services causes the need to re-educate all your employees and new hires. Which can partly be seen as a network effect, but which also brings us neatly to the next example: high switching costs.

If **switching costs** for customers are high, it provides a high "customer lock-in". Which means that even if you increase your prices drastically, clients will keep buying your products. Having to retrain your workforce to switch from AutoCAD to Rhino comes with a cost. But also the implementation of software can be an expensive exercise. Think about ERP systems, or products like Salesforce: they are built into the core of many systems. Changing to a competitor causes huge costs to implement the new software. And on top of that, it adds the risk of errors in the implementation. If that can cause a temporary shutdown of your factory or production line, the associated costs—and the loss of consumer confidence for not delivering your products in time—can be huge. Therefore, there will be a tendency to avoid the risk and the pain of switching to a different provider, even if it means paying slightly higher prices every year...

Operational leverage

Operational leverage is another quality one looks for in a company. Because the best companies benefit from positive economies of scale: they grow, and the larger they get, the lower the marginal cost becomes to deliver the product or service. Which translates in the financial statements as follows: **For great companies, the lower one gets on the income statement, the higher the percentage growth rate becomes.** For example, a 3% increase in revenue translates into a 5% increase in gross profit, an 8% increase in operating profit, and a 12% increase in net profit. And if the company bought back some shares, this might even lead to a 13% increase in earnings per share.

The reason behind this is simple: for a company with operational leverage, the same equipment can be used at a higher utilization rate, meaning the cost of producing an additional item gets cheaper the higher the volumes get. Larger volumes might also give the company more leverage in its negotiations with suppliers, decreasing costs on a per-unit basis. This, in turn, leads to an increase in gross profits. Other costs, like marketing, administration, and other overhead costs are predominantly fixed and do not scale to the same extent as sales does. So if larger sales numbers are obtained, these "fixed" costs can be spread over more units of production, leading to lower operating costs per unit, or thus operating profits increasing at a larger percentage rate than gross profit did.

For good companies, this increase in operating profits translates in good cash inflows, which means debt can be paid down and interest coverage ratios improve. Both of these lead to better financing terms and lower interest expenses, which increases the net profit even more than the operating profit improved.

Companies that consistently show this type of profile in the earnings statement are an equity investor's dream and retirement savings plan. At least as long as the company can keep growing.

Unfortunately, it often also works the other way around. If—because of increased competition or because of an economic downturn—revenue declines, it can lead to a way bigger decrease on the bottom line of the income statement too. Many production companies share these characteristics: They require expensive equipment, leading to high fixed costs regardless of utilization rates. So when the market expands, higher utilization rates reduce per-unit production costs, resulting in strong financial statements that make the business appear highly desirable. But it is important to notice that this is only the case at times when demand is growing. In a mature market, or in an economic downturn, demand decreases. But the equipment keeps depreciating, and stopping production lines might be expensive, or even impossible, in certain industries. So in an economic downturn, all too often these levers becomes pincers: a small decrease in revenue leads to a much larger decrease of net profits, causing pain to the company and its investors[15].

This is why **the perfect company is a growing company, with macro-economic tailwinds** that keep lasting in the foreseeable future.

To a certain extent, this is also true for software companies. Developing a software product is expensive—a large fixed cost. But the incremental cost of selling an additional copy of the product essentially costs nothing at all. Leading to the same characteristics in the income statement. This is the case for products like video games, but also for music producers and platform providers. It is not true for software that needs a lot of customization and personalization per user: these companies have a lower operating leverage. However, even these software companies can often be superior compared to companies active in the heavy industry sectors, especially in economic downturn scenarios. This is because programmers can be laid off in times of recession, while the equipment in the factory keeps depreciating, and requiring maintenance.

---

[15] Furthermore, production companies have the disadvantage that lots of capital outlays are required to grow. This is a strong negative point. The reasons for this will be discussed in detail chapter 5.

Differentiated customer base

The perfect company has a wide customer base. Which means the dependency of each one of them is very limited. Think Coca-Cola: literally billions of clients drink Coke daily. So if the economy in one part of the world is slow, another region might offset this by growing above average. This provides balance and reduces the risk to a company like The Coca-Cola Company.

The extreme example on the other end is, for example, a large defense contractor. Lockheed Martin basically has one client: the American Department of Defense (DoD). Maybe that is a little bit exaggerated: they also sell to other nations. But not by much: the US, their primary client, has to give explicit permission to Lockheed (and others) to do business with anyone else across the globe. While this can be a blessing in times the budget of that one client is increasing, it also implies an above average risk if things go the other way around, and if that client's budget comes under pressure. Or if the relationships with that single client sours. So the perfect company has a very wide customer base.

Another important aspect to take into consideration is the following question: Are your customers wealthy (for consumer companies), or making money (for b2b)? Luxury brands are famously stable during economic downturns: the real wealthy clients are often not really affected by economic hardship, or at least not to a level that they have to reduce their spending habits. While anyone from the upper middle class to the lower classes are affected by economic cycles: they depend on an income from labor and/or or the stock market to keep their spending habits up. So if the economy crash and layoffs hit, the middle (and lower) class have to cut back on spending, negatively affecting most companies providing services to them[16].

It is important to stress the distinction between a customer base of the very wealthy people versus the "aspirational riches": the first category is not affected by an economic crash. But the latter, often also named "luxury" or "affordable luxury," has clients who are in fact overspending their budgets in good times, to keep up appearances—and can be hit extremely severely when the economic cycle

---

[16] Not all of them though. Some companies, like dollar stores, might even profit during times of economic hardship. Because their customer base—low-budget customers—grows in size.

turns south. So if your client base is primarily the latter, you can expect serious boom-bust cycles, contrary to the real luxury segment. While in good times, they behave similarly. Which can make it sometimes surprisingly difficult to keep that distinction in mind. Anyway, your perfect b2c client is very wealthy.

For b2b companies, on the other hand, it is important to keep an eye on the profitability of your customers themselves. The b2b translation of "being wealthy" is "being profitable over long periods of time."

For example, car manufacturers (or more broadly, "Original Equipment Manufacturers" or OEMs) typically have very low profit margins. As a supplier to those companies, you can expect that price negotiations will be very fierce at every contract discussion: Paying slightly too much compared to competitors might be the difference between (corporate) life and dead for the OEM. On the other hand, if your customer is making large profits, and has high profit margins himself, they might not care that much about the price. If LVMH buys in leather for their Louis Vuitton handbags, I'm sure there will be negotiations in which price plays a role. But given the high profit margins, and the relative unimportance of the leather cost to the total selling price of the product, quality and timely delivery of the goods might get priority, even if it means they knowingly pay slightly higher prices.

Another point to notice: delivering a small part to companies can be more financially gratifying than delivering important goods. A small expense is, for large companies, often not worth the time negotiating over. They might even skip comparing your product with the products of lots of different vendors.

For example, margins on laptops are often low: Dell realizes an operating margin of around 6%. Margins on headsets, mice and accessories are often larger: Logitech realizes operating margins in the neighborhood of 14%, or more than double of what Dell realizes.

WD-40 is, once again, a nice example: on top of being a recognizable brand name, they sell a relatively cheaper product, small oil sprays, to avoid anti-oxidation on more expensive machinery. Very few people want to risk causing damage to the expensive equipment, in order to save a couple of cents on something that is inexpensive in the grander scheme of things. So for a lot of clients, buying oil sprays from a different brand is often just not worth the risk. Even if it means paying 10, 25, or even 50 cents more for the same product. But on a purchase of 5 USD, 50 cents means a revenue increase of 10%. Which goes straight through to the bottom line of the company (except for taxes payable on the higher profit). So a 10% increase in revenue might mean the profitability of the company is 50% higher than a competitor with lesser known brands.

Differentiated supplier base

On the supplier side, the same is true: you don't want to be too dependent on a limited number of suppliers. Preferably, you can choose between a wide number of suppliers who deliver very similar products, which allows you to negotiate more heavily on price, leading to lower costs, and more favorable payment terms. **The perfect company has a wide and differentiated supplier base**

An example of companies that have both good customer bases and good supplier bases are the beverage manufacturers. Beer giant AB InBev has, for most aspects of making beer, lots of different suppliers to choose from. And on the supplier side, they have lots of different pubs as clients, all around the globe, which enables them to discuss very favorable terms of the trade on both ends.

It also worth inverting the example and looking at your company from the other side of the negotiating table. On the supplier end, AB InBev is a large and important customer for producers of glass bottles from companies like Verallia and O-I Glass, and even more so for farmers growing hops. Which gives the beer giant ample negotiating power to drive down the price of their supplies. On the other hand AB InBev's clients, the pub owners, cannot afford to not offer AB InBev products. Not having these products on their menu will cost pubs beer-drinking clients. So as a pub owner, you kind of have to accept whatever price and payment terms AB InBev asks for. (It's similar for Coca-Cola, to name another example in the beverage industry.)

Another aspect to take into consideration is the dependency on commodities. Prices of oil, gold, and even copper or steel can vary widely over short periods of time. If commodities make up a large part of your sales price, the question becomes how easily you can pass through those costs to your end customers. If this can be done easily, and if sales volumes are also not expected to drop too much when prices increase, that's OK (e.g. oil refineries, which hold low inventories of oil, and can pass through prices of refined oil products almost immediately to their end customers). If, on the other hand, you hold lots of inventory, cannot fully pass through commodity prices to your end customer, or increased prices have a large effect on order volumes, then your business line is not as good.

For example, companies that build truck trailers need lots of steel. But if steel prices increase, a number of things are likely to happen:

- Steel prices cannot be fully passed through to end customers immediately, affecting profit margins[17].
- More money will be locked up in inventory, because the same amount of steel is now more costly.
- Demand for truck trailers is likely going to decrease in the short to middle run, because of those higher prices.

All of them have a negative impact on the business. Making such companies, like Wabash National, for example, very vulnerable to steel prices.

A limited set of competitors

It is better to have a limited set of competitors: a monopoly would be perfect, although an oligopoly can work just fine too. However, you want to avoid a too fragmented set of competitors, in which there is always at least one of them trying to win market share by undercutting your prices.

The theory taught at Harvard is that generally only the top two or three companies in a sector can make money. So the ideal company is a market leader in a growing niche. But even then, it is better to be a market leader with only two or three other players that behave in a price-disciplined way, than to have many small competitors trying to nibble on your market share.

---

[17] Although initially, accounting profit margins will increase. Because trailers can be sold at higher prices, while the steel sold to produce them is in the books at the earlier, lower steel prices. This is only a temporary effect though. And the analyst should recognize that the increase in profit margins is not caused by an increase in pricing power, but is soon to be (more than) reversed once the "cheaper inventory" left the building. So don't be fooled by the initial hike in accounting profitability!

Furthermore, the more limited the number of competitors generally means the more limited innovation is too, which is an important advantage for companies (and their shareholders) as well, especially if the moat of the company is technology-based. A business in which one needs to keep reinventing himself to stay alive is a more difficult business compared to a sector without any innovation.

A cheap stock price

Last but not least, obviously, you want to pay as low a price as possible for owning a piece of your great business, meaning your earnings yield is as high as possible. **The perfect company can be acquired at a cheap price.**

The perfect company... does not exist

While the idea of finding the *perfect* company is appealing, it is crucial to acknowledge that such a company simply does not exist. However, just because a business falls short of perfection does not mean its stock is never worth buying— it simply means that the price you pay should reflect its imperfections. For example, a high-quality software giant like Microsoft may justify a higher earnings multiple than a more cyclical, capital-intensive company like Wabash National, a truck trailer manufacturer. This doesn't mean Wabash is always a poor investment or that Microsoft is always a great one. But if both trade at the same multiple of their through-the-cycle earnings power, Microsoft would likely be the superior choice.

At the same time, price matters. Ideally, you want to acquire a great business at the lowest possible price, maximizing your earnings yield. The perfect scenario is finding a high-quality company trading cheaply, but that shouldn't be the absolute priority at the expense of everything else. As Warren Buffett wisely put it, *"It is way better to buy a wonderful company at a fair price than to buy a fair company at a wonderful price."* No matter how strong a business is, overpaying for its stock can lead to disappointing returns. But quality is just as important as valuation. After all, an investment in the equity of a struggling company that goes broke is a terrible investment, no matter how cheap its stock appeared to be.

The balance between price and quality is where the best investment decisions are made.

Chapter Summary

In this chapter, it was explained that the perfect company has a moat around its business model, which means that competitors cannot easily target your clients. Companies can have a moat because of:

- a technological advantage
- regulatory grants, such as patents and licenses
- branding
- network effects
- customers having high switching costs when abandoning your product in favor of a competitor's offering.

The perfect company is active in a growing sector and faces natural tailwinds, and on top of that, enjoys a high operating leverage, which means its profits increase at a faster rate than its revenue increases.

Furthermore, the perfect company has a wide supplier base, and a wide customer base. Whereas ideally this is not the case the other way around, meaning you are an important supplier for your customers, and an important client for your supplier. And it doesn't take a rocket scientist to understand that the perfect company does not have a lot of competitors.

Ideally, such companies can be bought at a cheap stock price. In reality, trade-offs are to be made. The closer a company gets to the description of "the perfect company," the higher the price one can afford to pay for its stock.

CHAPTER 5

Valuation

> *"The stock market is filled with individuals who know the price of everything, but the value of nothing."*
>
> – Philip Fisher

In the previous sections, it was mentioned a couple of times that one wants to buy stocks "cheaply" or "below their intrinsic value". But what is cheap? And what is the correct way to compare the valuation of companies? In this section, we will dive into the valuation exercise.

In chapter 3, it was explained that while the DCF-model is a useful theoretical framework and a good exercise to think about the valuation of projects, its practical usability in stock analysis remains very limited. Due to its sensitivity to small changes in input parameters, and its requirement to estimate accurate numbers far away in an all too uncertain future. So the DCF-model doesn't bring the analyst much further.

A more useful tool in the toolbox of the financial analyst is ratios and multiples. Because stock picking and asset allocation is a relative exercise: you want the best performing, fastest growing or cheapest valued stock of your investable universe. Ratios allow you to compare the valuation and the operational performance of a company with those of peers: competitors and alternative investments. A comparison between the closest competitors in a sector helps to determine which stock to buy in that sector. But comparing different companies in different sectors can also be useful, in order to get a grasp on how interesting a sector as a whole is to invest in. And comparing the current multiples with those of the company's own history can also provide some useful insights and give a feel of whether the company is currently attractively valued.

The first and most important question is: which ratios to look at. When analyzing a ratio, it is important to know the strengths and shortcomings of each

// VALUATION

of them. Unfortunately, there is no holy grail, and the ones most often used in journals, even financial ones, are often the most misleading. In the next section, some of these pitfalls will be highlighted, and the uses and limitations of various ratios will be discussed.

Strengths and Pitfalls of the Price/Earnings Ratio

When is the P/E ratio useful?

Let's start with the most widely known and used one: the price-earnings ratio. The biggest advantage is its simplicity: just divide the share price by the earnings per share the company generates. Easy.

The ratio is also easy to understand: its inverse gives you the earnings yield. Pay 1,000 USD for a company that generates 80 USD of profit annually, and you have a P/E of 12.5, or an earnings yield of 8%. Assuming a steady state situation in which there is no inflation and no growth, then that 8% is indeed the return the company will generate for you every year, which can, for example, be paid out as a dividend.

As an example—which will be used throughout this chapter—assume a company with the following financial statements, as given in the tables below. The net sales equals 1,000 USD. Gross profits of 600 USD imply a gross margin of 60%. Selling, General and Administrative (SG&A) costs amount to 200 USD per year, and Research and Development (R&D) expenses amount to 175 USD, leading to an EBITDA (Earnings Before Interest, Taxes, Depreciation and Amortization) of 225 USD. Depreciation and Amortization of 125 USD per year leads to an EBIT (Earnings Before Interest and Taxes) of 100 USD. For simplicity, in this example the company is all equity-financed, so interest expenses are zero. A 20% tax rate converts the 100 EBIT into a net profit of 80 USD.

As one assumes no inflation and no growth in this first example, it also means that both the sales price and costs remain flat. This assumes that capital expenditures equal the depreciation expenses. The company needs 1,000 USD of fixed assets to be able to produce these results, and is all equity financed. One gets the following financial statements:

Income Statement	Year 1	Year 2	Year 3	Year 4	Year 5
Sales	1,000	1,000	1,000	1,000	1,000
COGS	- 400	- 400	- 400	- 400	- 400
Gross profit	600	600	600	600	600
SG&A, excl. D&A	- 200	- 200	- 200	- 200	- 200
R&D	- 175	- 175	- 175	- 175	- 175
EBITDA	225	225	225	225	225
Depreciation & Amortization	- 125	- 125	- 125	- 125	- 125
EBIT (= EBT)	100	100	100	100	100
Income tax	- 20	- 20	- 20	- 20	- 20
Net profit	80	80	80	80	80

Free Cash Flow Calculation	Year 1	Year 2	Year 3	Year 4	Year 5
Net profit	80	80	80	80	80
Depreciation & Amortization	125	125	125	125	125
CapEx	- 125	- 125	- 125	- 125	- 125
FCF	80	80	80	80	80
Dividend paid out	- 80	- 80	- 80	- 80	- 80
Added to Retained Earnings	-	-	-	-	-

VALUATION

Simplified Balance Sheet	Year 0	Year 1	Year 2	Year 3	Year 4	Year 5
Cash	-	-	-	-	-	-
Productive Assets	1,000	1,000	1,000	1,000	1,000	1,000
Total Assets	1,000	1,000	1,000	1,000	1,000	1,000
Liabilities	-	-	-	-	-	-
Shareholders' Equity	1,000	1,000	1,000	1,000	1,000	1,000
Total Liabilities & Stockholders' Equity	1,000	1,000	1,000	1,000	1,000	1,000

If the company trades at a P/E of 12.5, then the company is exactly worth its book value of 1,000 USD. If the company trades at 2,000 USD, however, its P/E ratio would be 25 (25*80 = 2,000). The yearly earnings would still be 80, so the equity holder would be getting an earnings yield of 4% on his or her money.

Obviously, the lower the P/E ratio—and the higher its inverse, the earnings yield—the better.

Why the Price/Earnings ratio is less useful than you think

Unfortunately, its popularity hides a number of shortcomings of the P/E ratio. We'll focus on two:

▸ The inability to take into account the capital structure of the company, which can lead to misleading conclusions when comparing companies with different debt levels.
▸ Its disregard for the capital intensity of a sector, or the assets needed to create the revenue, and the additional capital needed to generate growth.

Difference in capital structure

To illustrate this point, compare the following two companies. EquityCo and DebtCo. EquityCo is, as its name implies, all equity financed, and has the financial statements described in the previous section. DebtCo has 600 USD of debt on the balance sheet, on which a 5% interest rate is to be paid. Besides this, everything else is identical to EquityCo. DebtCo produces the following financial statements:

Income Statement	Year 1	Year 2	Year 3	Year 4	Year 5
Sales	1,000	1,000	1,000	1,000	1,000
COGS	- 400	- 400	- 400	- 400	- 400
Gross profit	600	600	600	600	600
SG&A, excl D&A	- 200	- 200	- 200	- 200	- 200
R&D	- 175	- 175	- 175	- 175	- 175
EBITDA	225	225	225	225	225
Depreciation & Amortization	- 125	- 125	- 125	- 125	- 125
EBIT	100	100	100	100	100
Interest	- 30	- 30	- 30	- 30	- 30
EBT	70	70	70	70	70
Income tax	- 14	- 14	- 14	- 14	- 14
Net profit	56	56	56	56	56

Free Cash Flow Calculation	Year 1	Year 2	Year 3	Year 4	Year 5
Net profit	56	56	56	56	56
Depreciation & Amortization	125	125	125	125	125
CapEx	- 125	- 125	- 125	- 125	- 125
FCF	56	56	56	56	56
Dividend paid out	- 56	- 56	- 56	- 56	- 56
Added to Retained Earnings	-	-	-	-	-

Simplified Balance Sheet	Year 0	Year 1	Year 2	Year 3	Year 4	Year 5
Cash	-	-	-	-	-	-
Productive Assets	1,000	1,000	1,000	1,000	1,000	1,000
Total Assets	1,000	1,000	1,000	1,000	1,000	1,000
Liabilities	600	600	600	600	600	600
Shareholders' Equity	400	400	400	400	400	400
Total Liabilities & Stockholders' Equity	1,000	1,000	1,000	1,000	1,000	1,000

The net profit of DebtCo is lower: 56 USD, versus the 80 USD generated by EquityCo. Because DebtCo has to pay 30 USD interest per year (5% interest on a 600 USD loan). Here's a question: If the share price of EquityCo is 1,000, and the share price of DebtCo is 400, which company is the cheaper one?

Based on the P/E ratio, one would tend to opt for DebtCo, which trades at a P/E of 7.1 (400/56), while EquityCo trades at a P/E of 12.5 (= 1,000/80). The correct answer, however, is that they are the same company! If EquityCo decides to take on 600 of debt (and assuming 5% is a market conform interest rate) and pay this out to its shareholders as a one-off dividend, its financial statements become the one of DebtCo. And the price paid for the company is also equal: 1,000 minus the 600 in dividends received equals 400, which is what one had to pay for DebtCo. So they are literally the same company. They should be worth the same because no value can be created out of thin air by just opting for a different financing structure at market conform rates[18]. So one needs to conclude that **the P/E ratio is very misleading when comparing companies with different capital structures.**

---

[18] This is almost, but not entirely true. Interest-deductibility creates a small tax-advantage to add debt financing. See the Modigliani-Miller theorem. Furthermore, adding debt can create a bit more pressure on the management of the company to keep costs under control, as debt covenants must be met. A more detailed discussion on this topic can be found in later chapters.

BEYOND THE NOISE

A better measure to compare companies with a different capital structure is the EV/EBIT ratio. More on the EV/EBIT later on, but one can already spot that the EV/EBIT for both companies equals 10: an enterprise value of 1,000 (1,000 in equity + 0 debt for EquityCo, and 400 equity + 600 debt for Debtco), and EBIT equals 100 for both companies. But before we move on the the EV/EBIT ratio, let's first return to the EquityCo example, and see what happens if a bit of growth is added to the equation.

Difference in Capital Intensity

Let's revisit the example of EquityCo. But now, assume the company reinvests the money to grow, instead of just paying out all profits as a dividend. To keep things as simple as possible, we'll keep ignoring inflation.

In this example, one assumes the full net profit is used to buy assets, accounted for in Property, Plant and Equipment (PP&E) on the balance sheet, and is depreciated via straight-line depreciation. We assume a useful life of 15 years for the equipment, and assume the company was performing in a steady state in the past, which implies the average asset on the balance sheet is 8 years old. This is made a bit more tangible in the table below: Assume the company has 15 product lines, with equipment per line worth 125 USD when bought new. Given the straight-line depreciation, this gives the following depreciation schedule and assets:

Equipment Purchase Year	Price When Bought New	Book Value of the Equipment
Equipment bought 14 years ago	125	8
Equipment bought 13 years ago	125	17
Equipment bought 12 years ago	125	25
Equipment bought 11 years ago	125	33
Equipment bought 10 years ago	125	42
Equipment bought 9 years ago	125	50
Equipment bought 8 years ago	125	58
Equipment bought 7 years ago	125	67
Equipment bought 6 years ago	125	75
Equipment bought 5 years ago	125	83

// VALUATION

Equipment bought 4 years ago	125	92
Equipment bought 3 years ago	125	100
Equipment bought 2 years ago	125	108
Equipment bought 1 year ago	125	117
Equipment bought this year	125	125
Total Gross PP&E	1,875	
Total Net PP&E		1,000

So the total gross PP&E equals 1,875 and the net book value of the PP&E equals 1,000.

Now, instead of paying out the earnings of the first year as a dividend, the company opts to reinvest its profits: it buys new equipment. So after year 1, the company made 80 profit, which is used to buy additional new equipment. Under the assumption that all equipment is performing equally (regardless of age), this will allow it to increase the volumes of produced goods by 80/1875 = 4.27%. Assuming the additional products can be sold at equal prices, and assuming all costs remain the same (as a percentage of revenue). And assuming the new machine also gets written down on a straight line, which increases the depreciation charges as well.

One gets the following financial statements:

Income Statement	Year 1	Year 2	Year 3	Year 4	Year 5
Sales	1,000	1,043	1,087	1,134	1,182
COGS	- 400	- 417	- 435	- 453	- 473
Gross profit	600	626	652	680	709
SG&A, excl D&A	- 200	- 209	- 217	- 227	- 236
R&D	- 175	- 182	- 190	- 198	- 207
EBITDA	225	235	245	255	266
Depreciation & Amortization	- 125	- 130	- 136	- 142	- 148
EBIT (= EBT)	100	104	109	113	118
Income tax	- 20	- 21	- 22	- 23	- 24
Net profit	80	83	87	91	95

BEYOND THE NOISE

Balance Sheet & Returns	Year 0	Year 1	Year 2	Year 3	Year 4	Year 5
Cash	-	-	-	-	-	-
Productive Assets	1,000.00	1,080.00	1,163.41	1,250.39	1,341.07	1,435.62
Total Assets	1,000.00	1,080.00	1,163.41	1,250.39	1,341.07	1,435.62
Liabilities	-	-	-	-	-	-
Shareholders' Equity	1,000.00	1,080.00	1,163.41	1,250.39	1,341.07	1,435.62
Total Liabilities & Stockholders' Equity	1,000.00	1,080.00	1,163.41	1,250.39	1,341.07	1,435.62
Return on Assets (= Return on Equity)	-	8.0%	7.7%	7.5%	7.3%	7.1%

Now compare this to another company that has the same profit margins but has a higher capital intensity. E.g. assume the following company:

Category	Year 1	Year 2	Year 3	Year 4	Year 5
Sales	1,000	1,021	1,043	1,065	1,088
COGS	- 275	- 281	- 287	- 293	- 299
Gross profit	725	740	756	772	789
SG&A, excl D&A	- 200	- 204	- 209	- 213	- 218
R&D	- 175	- 179	- 183	- 186	- 190
EBITDA	350	357	365	373	381
Depreciation & Amortization	- 250	- 255	- 261	- 266	- 272
EBIT (= EBT)	100	102	104	107	109
Income tax	- 20	- 20	- 21	- 21	- 22
Net profit	80	82	83	85	87

// VALUATION

	Year 1	Year 2	Year 3	Year 4	Year 5
Gross PP&E (before reinvestment)	3,750	3,830	3,912	3,995	4,080
Cumulative depreciation	- 1750	- 1755	- 1766	- 1782	- 1804
Invested capital	2,000	2,075	2,146	2,213	2,276

	Year 1	Year 2	Year 3	Year 4	Year 5
Net profit	80	82	83	85	87
Depreciation & Amortization	250	255	261	266	272
Maintenance CapEx	- 250	- 255	- 261	- 266	- 272
FCF	80	82	83	85	87
Price of new equipment	250	250	250	250	250
Extra equipment	0.32	0.33	0.33	0.34	0.35

This company makes the same 1,000 USD revenue and generates the same net profit margin of 8%. However, to do so, it nets 2,000 USD worth of equipment, double of the company in our original example.

If this company now wants to use its proceeds to grow, it can invest the same 80 USD of net profit. However, this only leads to an increase of equipment of 2.13%: The asset base can only be expanded by 80/3,750 for this company, versus the 80/1,875 for the "capital light" company. So the company can only grow organically at half the speed of the first one.

If both companies trade at a P/E of 10, would you really be indifferent about which company to own? Or is one a more qualitative business than the other, and thus deserve a higher multiple? Obviously the capital-light business is preferred to the capital-intensive business. But this difference in **capital intensity of the business is not taken into account by the P/E ratio**, which is another shortcoming of this ratio.

It is really appalling to see how popular the use of P/E is, despite its obvious shortcomings. On the positive, it means if you made it this far in this book, your financial knowledge is already ahead of 70% of retail investors. (*Who said beating the markets is difficult?*)

> **Side Note:**
>
> Some readers might be wondering why the "capital light" company is only growing at 4.27%, and not at 8%. Because the company reinvested 80, and its assets have a book value of 1,000. Yet the assumed growth rate in the example is only 80/1,875 = 4.27%.
>
> Why on 1,875, and not on 1,000? Because new equipment is to be bought at the price of new equipment, not at the average price of the equipment that is currently on the books.
>
> | | Year 1 | Year 2 | Year 3 | Year 4 | Year 5 |
> |---|---|---|---|---|---|
> | Gross PP&E (before reinvestment) | 1,875 | 1,955 | 2,038 | 2,125 | 2,216 |
> | Cumulative depreciation | -875 | -880 | -891 | -908 | -931 |
> | Invested capital | 1,000 | 1,075 | 1,147 | 1,217 | 1,285 |
>
> It's like every year for the last 15 years, 1 machine worth 125 USD was bought. Given the straight-line depreciation, the oldest machine is in the books for 8, while the newest is still worth 125. Now we buy additional equipment for 80. So 80/125th of a new machine can be bought. (Assuming fractional machines give the proportional output.)
>
> So instead of 15 machines producing 1,000 USD of revenue, we now have 15 + 80/125 = 15.64 machines, producing 15.64/15.00*1,000 = 1,043 USD of revenue.
>
> Real life is obviously more complicated than this simplified example. Newer machines might be performing better, older machines might need more maintenance and cause for more frequent *"unscheduled maintenance"* (which is management talk for "breaking down"). But most often, the concept still stands. Which means that fast-growing companies look less performant on their asset base (lower Return on Assets or RoA), because their equipment is newer, and thus for a higher value in the books.

> This once again highlights how easily accounting standards can be misleading. Crunching the numbers and calculating financial ratios is the simple part. But correctly interpreting what they truly signify is where the real challenge lies!

EV/ EBIT

As already touched upon in the previous section, the EV/EBIT ratio is better at comparing the valuation of companies with vastly different debt levels. Loosely speaking, the difference between P/E and EV/EBIT is that:

- the EV/EBIT ratio takes into account the profits for all stakeholders. Being the equity holders, the debt holders, and the taxman.
- the P/E ratio only takes into account the profits attributable to the equity holders.

When looking to invest in the equity of a company, the reflex is to look at the P/E, because it is only the net profit that is attributable to the equity holder. But as we have seen in the previous chapter, this complicates comparing similar companies with different debt profiles. Because companies with a higher indebtedness are riskier, their "fair P/E ratio" drops when debt levels increase. By how much? That is difficult to quantify exactly, and also does not follow a linear pattern. Therefore, an easier solution is to value the company as a whole, and thus look at EV/EBIT, after which the value of the debt is deducted to arrive at a fair equity value.

Another advantage of this approach is that it allows you to value the returns generated by the business as a whole, compared to bonds and more risk-free assets. To explain this, let's go back to another example.

Assume a debt-free company with the following (simplified) earnings statements[19]:

Revenue		100
COGS	-	40
Gross profit		60
SG&A	-	20
R&D	-	10
EBIT		30
Interest		-
EBT		30
Tax	-	6
Net profit		24

---

[19] We'll ignore debt and inflation to simplify the example.

Assuming that the company can keep generating the same profits every year, what is the company worth? Am I willing to buy this company for 200 USD? 500 USD? 1,000 USD? Well, the answer to every question in this book is: "It depends". Everything must be measured against something else. Nothing is of any value in a vacuum, so every investment is to be measured against an alternative set of investments[20].

The easiest comparable is the return offered by US government bonds. Because this is a good proxy of what returns a "safe" investment is offering.

If the stock is currently trading at 300 USD, this means the company is trading at 10x EV/EBIT (300/30), or 12.5x net earnings after tax (300 / 24). Which means

- The company is able to generate a 10% pre-tax profit.
- The equity investor gets an 8% earnings yield on his investment, after taxes.

In a time where the "risk-free" government bonds yield is 3%, this would look like a good deal. If bond yields were 15%, this would be a terrible deal. So, as always and with everything in stock analysis, the answer is: *it depends…*

As a rule of thumb:

- Use 10-year US government bonds to determine the risk-free rate. For companies who are mainly earning their money in other currencies[21], use an equivalent of this. Make sure the bond yield is retrieved from as risk-free an institution as possible, and use bonds with a good liquidity.
- Based on historical estimates, the equity risk premium is 4.5% – 5.5%. In this book one will use 5% as the market risk premium.

---

[20] Remember the very first chapter of this book, in which it was stated that everyone has an asset allocation? Cash is also an asset, and not making an allocation decision is actually also making a decision. Everything is an asset (or a liability), and needs to be compared with all other possible choices…

[21] For non-US companies, listed in countries with different currencies, the general advice is to use the 10-year government bond yield of that region as a proxy for the risk-free rate. However, it is also important to look where the company has most of its production. E.g. for a company operating mainly in the US, but who is listed in the UK, an argument can be made to make the entire analysis in USD: convert the income statements from GBP to USD, and use American government bonds as proxy to estimate the risk-free rate. In reality, the opposite is more frequent. E.g. European companies listing in the US. Convert everything to EUR, and use the 10y EU government bonds of the country with the lowest yield as an estimation for the EUR risk-free rate.

// VALUATION

So in current market conditions, with the government bond yield around 5%, you want to add 5% market risk premium, so a 10% yield is what you are looking for. Meaning you are willing to pay 10x EBIT (EV/EBIT = 10) for a non-growing company. So one should be willing to pay about 300 USD for the equity of company A.

Looking at peers and at historical multiples can enhance your confidence when determining a "fair" multiple.

> **About the market risk premium.**
>
> Theoretical professors still teach the CAPM-model. Which suggests that you look at the volatility of the stock price, relative compared to the volatility of the market as a whole. And calculate the so-called "*beta*" of the stock. If the beta equals 1, your stock has an average market risk, so a risk premium of 5% is to be used. However, if the stock is very volatile, and fluctuates twice as much as the market as a whole (a beta of 2), the CAPM model states that you should use a risk premium of 2 x 5% = 10%.
>
> We do not agree with this theory. In an ideal world it would make sense, but this theory makes the implicit assumptions that:
>
> ▸ The volatility of the stock remains constant over time. Which is often not the case.
> ▸ And, more importantly, that the volatility of the stock price is a good measure of risk. Which is incorrect. If you are a long-term investor, high fluctuations of the stock price in the short term are irrelevant. What matters is the predictability of the earnings (and growth) of the company in the more distant future.
> If stock price fluctuations would be a good reflection on potential fluctuations of the future earnings of a company, then market price fluctuations would be a good proxy. But in practice, all too often this is absolutely not the case. Stock prices fluctuate based on the favors and flavors of the day. And prices of companies with very stable prospects sometimes fluctuate wildly. While their relationship to the long-term risk of the company is often low.

The question then becomes: how does one compensate for the risk of a company for which the earnings fluctuate widely over time? This is a harder one to solve. And at the same time the answer is elegantly easy: don't. It is always an option to simply stay away from such companies. One has the choice between thousands and thousands of listed companies to invest in. Why look to companies that are extremely hard to value? Furthermore, if their earnings fluctuate widely over time, not only is it difficult to predict the earnings over the next one or two years, it is also an indication that the company doesn't really have a moat, or pricing power. Otherwise, they would be able to keep revenue and profit margins more stable over time! So one piece of advice: if the company is too hard to predict, just stay away from it. There are literally thousands of listed stocks. Why make life harder than necessary?

That being said, the EV/EBIT ratio is also not the holy grail, because as an equity holder, the investor is mainly interested in his fair share of the profit. And EBIT is not it: Debt holders and the tax man are to be paid first, and only the remainder is attributable to the stockholder.

- Consider two equal companies, but one is operating in a low tax country, while the other is operating in a high tax rate country. Obviously the first one is more valuable to the stockholders. But EBIT does not take this into account at all.
- A second aspect is that the interest rates at which a company is financed play a role as well. Assume two companies with the same debt. But one was a savvy negotiator and managed to get a bank loan at a 5% interest rate, while the other one signed an agreement paying 7% for its loan (either by being a poorer negotiator, or by initiating the loan at a time when interest rates were still higher). The first company is obviously worth more to its stockholders than the second one. But this doesn't show in the EV/EBIT ratio, as interest is added back to the profits in the calculation of the EBIT.

  This, however, can be corrected for, by not taking the book value of the debt, but (an estimation of) the market value of the debt, to go from enterprise value to market value.

// VALUATION

Summary:

- The EV/EBIT ratio is the better measure to compare between companies.
- The P/E ratio is the better one to measure what the expected return is on your investment in a particular company.
- The holy grail does not exist. There is not a single ratio that has all the advantages and no drawbacks. (Otherwise investing would be too easy, wouldn't it?)

Growth, Inflation & Owner Earnings

In real life, companies evolve over time. So stock analysis shouldn't be limited to one picture: One should look at the entire movie because the evolution over time contains important information regarding the true value of a company. This means aspects like growth, but also capital allocations and reinvestment decisions are important elements to take into account when valuing a company, which is also where the balance sheet comes into play again.

Consider a railway company that can only grow its earnings by acquiring additional rails and trains. Compare this to a software company that requires close to zero additional costs to sell more of its load. Even if both companies have similar margins, profitability, and growth, if their P/E is equal, one should always prefer the capital light company. When stated like this, it is intuitive. But why? Well, basically because of two reasons: inflation and growth.

Growth is often only possible with additional investments. Which means a part of the net profit needs to be reinvested in the business. In our earlier example, if the railroad company wants to grow, additional tracks and trains need to be bought. Without external capital, this means the growth rate of the company is limited by the amount of money that can be reinvested in the business, or thus by the profit generated by the company. For a software company this is less often the case. If no client-specific software adjustments are needed, the company can in theory grow without limit. Selling additional software licenses doesn't cost the company additional means. In reality, often additional salespeople and marketing expenses will be needed to stir up demand. Which does cost money (and finding the right people can be the limiting factor determining the growth rate). A numeric example of this was already discussed earlier in this chapter and is a deficit in the use of the P/E ratio. The same is true for the EV/EBIT ratio: the capital intensity is not taken into account...

Another topic to discuss is **inflation**. In the toy examples given above, a stable economic environment was assumed, and the existence of inflation was neglected. How does the math change if inflation is introduced? In times of inflation, the depreciation—calculated based on the book value of equipment bought in the past—is an underestimation of the true replacement cost. Because the investments needed to just maintain the current level of operations are higher than the depreciation charge taken in the income statement, the net profit looks higher than it really is. Those reinvestments do need to be made, for the company to keep producing the same output volumes. Therefore, an improvement of the earnings formula is to not use the "Net Profit" or "EBIT" in the numerator, but instead look at the "Owner Earnings," calculated as follows:

Owner Earnings
$$= Net\ Profit + Depreciation\ and\ Amortization$$
$$- Maintenance\ CapEx$$
$$- additional\ working\ capital\ needs$$

The "owners' earnings" number is the profit the company can really spend, either on growth investments or distributions towards its shareholders.

And replacing "Net Profit" by "EBIT" in the formula above gives you the "*Owners EBIT*", which is useful to calculate an improved version of the EV/EBIT multiple.

Unfortunately, this introduces another level of complexity and judgement in the stock analysis. Depreciation and amortization charges can be found in the financial statements of the company. And although often a capex number is disclosed in the financial reporting as well, the maintenance capex is often not communicated. So estimates are required to guess what part of the capex is required to just maintain the current level of operations, and what part is "growth" capex to expand operations and grow the company.

One can't blame the management, or even financial reporting standards, for this. Most often it cannot be determined objectively which part is which, as new machinery is often introduced which both replaces the older version and is at the same time more efficient and increases the output of the production line. No "one-size-fits-all" formula can be given to give a good split-up between maintenance capex and growth capex. It all depends on the industry, and the type of investment, which is just one of the reasons that stock analysis is at least as much of an art as a science.

One thing still stands, though. The more "capital light" a company is, the lower the dollar amount of the underestimation will be between the reported depreciation and the maintenance capex.

Inflation

Note that there is no such a thing as "the inflation". There are always differences in inflation rates between different products. The inflation figures published by central banks and financial newspapers are an (often underestimated) average of the inflation of the entire economy.

In Chapter 1, we introduced the concept of the Porsche-Inflation, during which it was demonstrated that luxury goods appreciate quicker than other goods. If your company is in a business in which the end product appreciates quicker in value than the costs of your supplies, it means you managed to increase your margins. The opposite is also true: if your company can only pass through more modest price increases than its input cost increases, the result will be a suffering operating margin and reduced profitability.

Extra Tip: Since a company's ability to pass through inflation reflects its pricing power, examining how its profit margins fared during periods of high inflation can provide valuable insights about the quality and the strength of a business.

Another effect of inflation is that the growth of the company will appear larger than it really is. Because even with the same level of output, the revenue will grow with the inflation rate of the products sold. So don't get fooled by increasing growth figures in times of rising inflation. Keeping an eye on volumes sold, rather than net sales in hard currency, will help the savvy investor avoid that mistake.

A discussion about debt

A simplification that was swept under the rug in this chapter is the complication of the balance sheet. In the toy examples used above, a very simplified version of a balance sheet was used, which states only assets, shareholders' equity and liabilities. In reality, there are lots of different types of liabilities: sometimes clients help financing your assets. Think about supermarkets: clients pay cash at checkout, while the supermarket itself often has 30, 45 or even 60 days of payables outstanding to their suppliers. For example, at the time of writing (December 2024) the days payable outstanding at Walmart amounts to 43 days.

If the business grows, the company's payables, receivables, pension liabilities, et cetera will also scale. Thus, not the entire asset base needs to be financed by classical debt and equity. So the correct way of calculating debt levels is to make a split between "financing that requires a compensation", like bank loans, bonds (interest-bearing debt), and equity (for which the shareholder expects a rate of return, although not contractually binding) on the one hand, and non-interest bearing debt, like taxes payable, product warranty liabilities, customer payables, and the like. **Only subtract the compensation-bearing liabilities from your (fair value estimation of the) enterprise value to arrive at the fair market value of the equity.**

EBITDA and other adjustments to earnings figures

Earlier in this chapter, the P/E ratio and the EV/EBIT ratio were discussed, as well as the concept of owners' earnings. Out of which it should be fairly obvious that depreciation expenses are a real expense. Or if anything, even an underestimation of the true capital outlays required to maintain the current level of output, due to inflation. It goes without saying that investments are needed to replace old equipment over time.

Therefore, the widespread use of EBITDA as a measure in financial analysis blows our minds. Taking EBITDA into account gives a too rosy picture of reality and will favor capital intensive businesses in an unjustifiable way.

// VALUATION

Charlie Munger often made the following quote: **"I think that, every time you saw the word EBITDA, you should substitute the word 'bullshit earnings'. People who use EBITDA are either trying to con you or they're conning themselves."** We could not have said it any better. Limit the use of EV/EBITDA in your investment analysis as much as possible!

One exception, where EV/EBITDA can make sense, is for debtholders: The ratio can serve as a proxy of how much cash a company is able to generate, if the company would stop all investments in its future. E.g. if a credit crunch hits and the company preserves all cash it generates, how much would that be? As such, net debt over EBITDA is often used as a debt metric. That said, net debt / EBIT is also here the better metric for going concern companies, as it shows how quickly the company would be able to pay down its debt while reinvesting in equipment to keep current production levels where they are today.

Similarly, for other adjustments made to earnings statements, the question needs to be asked whether this is truly a one-off, or is more something that is part of doing business. For example, restructuring charges might fluctuate wildly from one year to the next. But excluding them entirely from the income statement gives too bright a picture of the true earnings power of the business: every once in a while, a cost-cutting exercise is necessary, and the costs related to layoffs, decommissioning of production lines, or even changing the management are true costs that need to be paid for. Using money coming from the company owners' pockets. (That means your pockets, sir!) So they need to be taken into account in the valuation of the equity!

On the other hand, taking large restructuring costs fully into account in one year is also too harsh, and gives too dark a picture of the company. The best advice we can give is to average these costs out over a number of years: Take the sum of those costs over the previous couple of years, and average them out over those years, to calculate an "average restructuring cost" per year. It will give a more realistic picture of the true long-term profit generating capabilities of the company. Over how many years should those costs be spread out? That depends on the company, and on how often those costs recur. Try to make a good guesstimation, to arrive at a realistic "average restructuring cost through the economic cycle." Stock analysis is more art than science, and this is just one of those parts where the art-part appears. There is no scientifically correct answer.

> **EBITDA: Earnings Before I Tricked the Dumb Auditor**
>
> ▸ **EBITDAC:** Earnings Before Interest, Taxes, Depreciation, Amortization, and Coronavirus.
> *(For those "once-in-a-lifetime" disruptions that lasted a bit longer.)*
> ▸ **EBITDAW**: Earnings Before Interest, Taxes, Depreciation, Amortization, and Weather.
> *(Blame the rain or heatwave for that missed target.)*
> ▸ **EBITDAB**: Earnings Before Interest, Taxes, Depreciation, Amortization, and Bitcoin.
> *(Because crypto gains and losses aren't "real," right?)*
> ▸ **EBITDAL**: Earnings Before Interest, Taxes, Depreciation, Amortization, and Lawsuits.
> *(Legal fees? What legal fees?)*
> ▸ **EBITDAPE**: Earnings Before Interest, Taxes, Depreciation, Amortization, and Poor Execution.
> *(It's not a failure, just a learning experience!)*
> ▸ **EBITDACR**: Earnings Before Interest, Taxes, Depreciation, Amortization, and CEO Replacements.
> *(Swapping leadership is a one-off, surely.)*
> ▸ **EBITDAS**: Earnings Before Interest, Taxes, Depreciation, Amortization, and Snacks.
> *(Because the free office snacks budget adds up.)*
> ▸ **EBITDAF**: Earnings Before Interest, Taxes, Depreciation, Amortization, and FOMO.
> *(The cost of keeping up with competitors.)*
> ▸ **EBITDARP**: Earnings Before Interest, Taxes, Depreciation, Amortization, and Really Poor Decisions.
> *(We swear this won't happen again.)*
> ▸ **EBITDAH**: Earnings Before Interest, Taxes, Depreciation, Amortization, and Hobbies.

VALUATION

(The CEO's golf club membership isn't really a business expense. Nor are half of the trips made with the corporate aircraft.)

- **EBITDAU**: Earnings Before Interest, Taxes, Depreciation, Amortization, and Unicorn Hunting.
  (Chasing that elusive billion-dollar valuation.)
- **EBITDAWW**: Earnings Before Interest, Taxes, Depreciation, Amortization, and "What Were We Thinking?"
  (That regrettable expansion into underwater real estate.)
- **EBITDAPJ**: Earnings Before Interest, Taxes, Depreciation, Amortization, and Pyjamas.
  (The remote work wardrobe upgrade wasn't free.)
- **EBITDAG**: Earnings Before Interest, Taxes, Depreciation, Amortization, and Gambling.
  (High-risk ventures? Let's just call them "bets.")
- **EBITDAM**: Earnings Before Interest, Taxes, Depreciation, Amortization, and Marketing.
  (Those Super Bowl ads weren't optional, we swear.)
- **EBITDAI**: Earnings Before Interest, Taxes, Depreciation, Amortization, and Inflation.
  (Because we didn't see that coming.)
- **EBITDAFW**: Earnings Before Interest, Taxes, Depreciation, Amortization, and Finger Wagging.
  (Regulators didn't really mean it.)
- **EBITDAWT**: Earnings Before Interest, Taxes, Depreciation, Amortization, and Wishful Thinking.
  (Optimistic projections shouldn't count against us!)

As a guide:

- Options expenses are a form of employee compensation and are to be considered a real cost.
- So are medical and retirement benefits.
- Litigation costs are real as well. But big fines or settlements can be averaged out over multiple year to give a more realistic "through-the-cycle" legal cost estimation.

- The same is true for fraud or hacking costs, and for disruptions caused by ERP-updates and that sort of "one-offs".
- Restructurings are often not a one-off. But also here, smoothing out certain expenses over multiple years can be acceptable in some cases.

Sometimes use EV/EBITA

The amortization of intangibles is a non-cashflow expense. Lots of companies present "adjusted earnings", which add back this amortization to the income. For some companies and some analysis, making this correction does make sense. In most situations, however, this can be classified as some sort of bull-created fertilizer, to manipulate earnings upwards.

Let's first have a look at situations when it does make sense to adjust for amortizations. For a company that did one large acquisition and is now paying down its debt, it can be very useful to see the "adjusted earnings" in which this non-cash expense is added back to the pre-tax income. Because the amortization is a non-cash outlay. And because the cash expense will not be repeated. So to calculate the true earnings power of the company, and its ability to quickly pay down the debt, the amortization expenses can be added back to the pre-tax profit.

The big difference between the amortization here, and the depreciation, which is also a "non-cash expense" but is not to be added back to earnings (and why one should avoid using EBITDA) is the following:

- In case of the amortization, one paid for the brand name, reputation and client lists of the acquired company. To sustain this, selling and marketing expenses will be made that are directly considered in the income statement as a cost. If the goodwill is written down too, one is actually counting the same expenditure twice.
- For equipment, this is not the case. The replacement of "old equipment", or capex, is added to the balance sheet, and written down as a depreciation expense over the years. If this depreciation expense is added back to the earnings, then the cost of the equipment is not taken into account anywhere!

// VALUATION

Also, if this adjustment for amortizations is not made, the profit of the company will take a jump the year the amortization is fully written down, which is completely artificial due to accounting standards.

However, for acquirers in industries in which the intangibles really have a defined "end date", these amortizations ARE to be taken into account. Think of pharmaceutical companies. Basically, those companies have to make a choice. Either they do all their research in-house, or they choose not to have a large research center, and just buy up small one-product biotech companies once they have FDA approval for their medicine, but before commercialization. (Most companies opt for a combination; partly own research, partly buying up patents, or biotech companies as a whole.) Only a small fraction of biotech research actually leads to an FDA-approved medicine. Let's simplify the numbers: assume the biotech company spends 100 million dollars on research and has a 1 in 10 chance of ending up with an approved product. Obviously, our large pharmaceutical company is not going to acquire a failed biotech. Only the company with the approved product gets an offer. A fair price (in this oversimplified toy example) would be to offer this company a cool billion USD. Of this amount, at least 900 million of it is pure goodwill. And probably even more than that, because part of the research costs will be "soft skills", and not tangible things as labs and microscopes. So maybe even 980 million will be goodwill, and 20 million will be tangible assets. Now that 980 million USD will be written off over the remaining period of the patent. Assuming the patent lasts for 20 years, this would lead to an amortization of 49 million USD per year (and a depreciation of 1 million USD per year).

In their financial reporting, too many pharmaceutical companies publish headline adjusted earnings, in which this amortization is added back to the GAAP earnings, as if this is an expense that does not exist. However, this expense is very real, and was paid up front, when acquiring the biotech company. It's very similar to when a piece of hardware, such as a computer or a car is bought and written down.

Thus, taking this amortization expense as a very real expense is the only way to correctly compare pharmaceutical companies that buy their product line with the ones that developed products themselves: To develop the product, the company would have needed to spend not 100 million USD (the cost of the development of that actual product), but 1 billion USD. To run the development of 10 different products, of which one would succeed and result in an actual FDA-approved product that can be commercialized. In-house R&D would be a very real expense: your researchers need to be paid, and their salaries are real costs. So why would the decision to externalize the research all of a sudden lead to bumped-up earnings?[22]

Needless to say, this example is very simplified. It ignores optionality in research, synergies of developing multiple related products under one roof, the certainty of having a filled pipeline, amongst others. But the basic idea of when amortization is really a one-off cost, versus a regular way of doing business, should be obvious by now: One-offs can sometimes be added back, or smoothed out over a longer period of time. But if it concerns a repeating expense, that is not taken into account in other ways in the income statement, it should count as a real expense.

Chapter Summary

There is no such thing as "the perfect ratio" to compare the value of companies. Every ratio has its strengths and pitfalls.

- ▸ The P/E ratio shows the earnings yield that can be expected. But it does a poor job at comparing companies with different debt profiles, or across sectors requiring a different capital intensity.
- ▸ The EV/EBIT ratios does a better job in comparing companies with large differences in debt profile, because it looks at a "total company valuation", including the debtholders in both numerator and denominator. It also offers a fairer assessment to compare the earnings profile generated by a company versus other potential investments. However, also here the capital intensity is not taken into account.
- ▸ EV/EBITDA is a less useful measure, and has limited value in analyzing stock valuations. It does have some (minor) value when analyzing debt levels, in that it shows the upper bound of cash generation if the company would stop all investments (including replacement investments). But it can be misleading as a valuation metric, especially

---

[22] The author is slightly allergic to this kind of "count yourself rich" accounting. Is there any pharmaceutical company developing pills against this?

when comparing companies across sectors with a different capital intensity. Because depreciation – or the replacement cost of capital goods – is a real expense.

- When inflation is not negligible, depreciation and amortization expenses should be replaced by the true, actual replacement costs. And thus use "owner earnings" and "owners' EBIT" instead of the values retrieved by the accounting statements. Good estimations of true replacement costs are often not readily available though, and require analyst estimations.
- In some circumstances, it is better to use EV/EBITA: in case of large acquisitions and when the company keeps investing in the brand, goodwill shouldn't be written down. So adding back the amortizations is acceptable.
- In case of large "one-off" costs, the analyst has to make an assessment of how "exceptional" these costs really are. And average them out over longer time horizons, to get a better understanding of the real "through-the-cycle" earnings power of the company in question.

CHAPTER 6

M&A, Growth, and Capital Allocation

> *"Don't gamble! Take all your savings and buy some good stock and hold it till it goes up, then sell it. If it don't go up, don't buy it."*
>
> – WILL ROGERS

Everything in the economy is made on growth. The eighth world wonder, compounding, only works its wonders if the multiplication factor is higher than one. And compounding is what really drives future returns and stock gains.

Shrinking, on the other hand, is often made "artificially" expensive: in some jurisdictions (read: Europe), laid off employees need to be paid multiple months of salary (up to two years in Germany for long-term employees, for example). But also strikes from unions might pump up the price of restructuring exercises. And, of course, you also have the effect of economies of scale, which work in the wrong direction when shrinking. If utilization rates of machinery drop, the per-unit price becomes more inflated.

> **Value Trap**
>
> One can often find cheap-looking stocks in no-growth sectors. Especially in the beginning of a shrinking phase, companies active in such a sector still post a decent profitability. Hence their price/earnings or EV/EBIT ratios look attractive. Don't be fooled: as soon as the shrinking phase kicks up a gear, profits vanish into thin air, and all of a sudden the cheap-looking valuation of yesterday looks expensive when assessed against the earnings of tomorrow.

// M&A, GROWTH, AND CAPITAL ALLOCATION

> These stocks are called *"valuation traps"* and are to be avoided *at all costs*. Which is often easier said than done, because it is not always obvious at first sight which companies are going to be forced to shrink and restructure in the near future.
>
> Especially when using valuation screenings, one can expect to have an above-average number of such stocks in the "filtered selection". And the disappointing prospects often only come visible when diving deeper into the fundamentals of the company. So when analyzing stocks, be prepared to start analyzing lots of companies, and end up with a decision not to buy them.
>
> This is, in fact, the most frustrating aspect in the job of an equity analyst. Spending your week analyzing a dozen of companies, and coming to the conclusion that none of them is actually worth buying, is not exceptional. Stay patient and keep grinding though the list of stocks is the only advice to give in these situations...

Therefore, growing is of utmost importance in almost all companies. But how can growth be attained? There are many different kinds of growth:

- One can do more of the same, either organically or by buying up competitors. This is called horizontal integration. Especially in more fragmented markets, this can be a lucrative exercise.
- One can buy up suppliers and/or clients (the latter only in b2b businesses) and be more vertically integrated. Acceptable in some sectors, more difficult in others.
- Or one can buy up a completely unrelated company. If this is done frequently, the result is a conglomerate, which often turns out to be a waste of both time and resources. With the notable exception of Berkshire Hathaway, the investment vehicle of Warren Buffett...

In what follows, each of these types of acquisitions will be discussed. But let's start by focusing on the first example: doing more of the same, either by buying up competitors or by growing organically. Which one is best?

Horizontal Acquisitions

Is it better to grow organically, or to grow via M&A? The answer to that question should be obvious by now. Can you guess it? The answer is the same one as to just about any other question in this book: it depends!

Most people tend to think that **organic growth** is better. Which is not wrong in a lot of circumstances. E.g. if your company has factories that are not yet running at 100% capacity, growing organically will help you boost the utilization rates of the existing factory. This gives an operational leverage: fixed costs remain the same, and can be spread over a larger production output. So production costs per unit decrease, which leads to higher operating margins. Awesome!

However, when new production facilities are needed, growing organically will require a lot of time and planning. The company needs to have the space, permits might be required, building and construction always take longer than you'd expect, and recruiting people can also be a difficult task, especially when the economy is doing well (which means unemployment rates are low). So, it might be easier and faster to grow via relatively small, **bolt-on acquisitions**. By buying smaller companies, you add the production capacity and the people at once. Furthermore, you also acquire a bunch of existing customers, which may lead to cross-selling opportunities.

And from a financial perspective, depending on the price paid for the acquisition, the choice between buying more machines and factory space and recruiting people yourself, versus reaching the same end point via the acquisition of a smaller competitor, might not be all that different.

Furthermore, buying smaller companies also has acceptable to low integration costs. Whereas mergers between equals often give rise to cultural clashes and corporate politics, for smaller acquisitions these risks tend to be more manageable. Although every acquisition is a bit different and has some specificities, companies who grow by regularly buying-up smaller companies can review each acquisition and create some sort of playbook to be used for future acquisitions and integrations. Which can make the process of acquiring and integrating bolt-on acquisitions into a well-oiled machine. Those "serial acquirers" or buy-and-build companies often turn out to be good investments, on two conditions:

- One, management does not overpay, and focusses on profitable growth, rather than revenue growth. Companies focusing on growth for the sake of growth often end up with disastrous financial statements. The measure that counts is the earnings per share, not the total revenue...
- Two, management doesn't push the balance sheet too far over the edge. Becoming greedy and trying to make too many acquisitions, and thereby letting debt levels get out of control, is to be avoided. A disciplined target as maximum debt level, which is then paid down before the next acquisition is done, is often the key to success for serial acquirers. As a result, the debt profile of a company over time should follow a sawtooth profile.

It also helps to (slowly but surely) consolidate the industry without causing too many lengthy approval processes from antitrust authorities, because each individual acquisition is relatively small in size. But in aggregate, in certain markets it helps to increase market share, and with that, increase pricing power.

Sawtooth profile of debt

The sawtooth pattern in the graph represents the cyclical nature of a serial acquirer's debt ratio, driven by acquisitions and subsequent debt repayment.

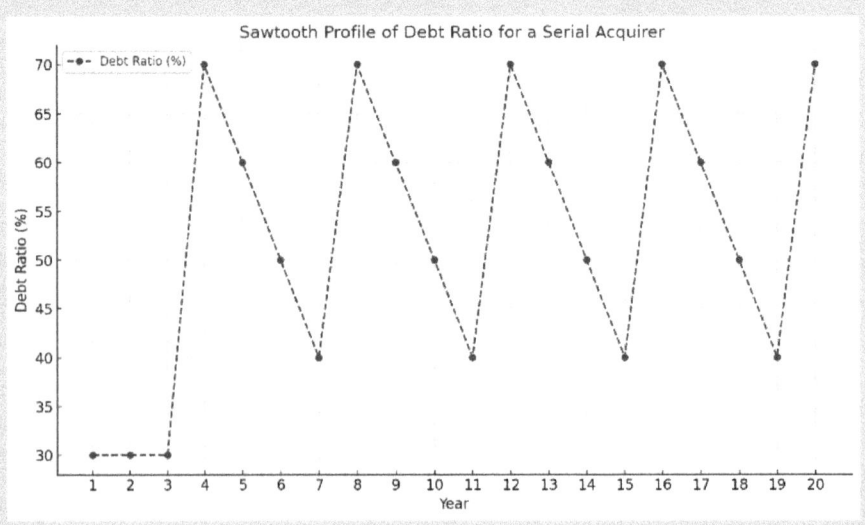

> The peaks (Rising Debt Ratio) occur when the serial acquirer undertakes a new acquisition. To fund acquisitions, companies often rely on debt financing, which significantly increases their debt ratio (total debt divided by equity or assets). The jump is sudden and reflects the large capital requirement of an acquisition.
>
> The declines (Falling Debt Ratio) occur after each acquisition. The company begins integrating the acquired business, aiming to generate additional cash flows from synergies or operational improvements. Over time, these cash flows are used to repay the debt incurred during the acquisition, leading to a gradual reduction in the debt ratio. The decline is more gradual than the rise, as debt repayment usually spans several years.
>
> The repetition of the cycle occurs because, once the debt ratio stabilizes after repayment, the serial acquirer pursues another acquisition, restarting the cycle and creating the next peak. This repetitive pattern of acquiring, repaying, and acquiring again forms the "sawtooth" profile seen in the graph.

Just as one example, "Installed Building Products," an American installer of—you guessed it—insulation and building products, acquired 88 companies over the last 10 years (2014-2023)[23] and over 200 companies since 1999. These were often smaller companies: in 2023 the company acquired 8 businesses that together generated 75 million USD revenue. But by following this strategy, the company was able to expand at a rapid pace, reaching 2.3 billion USD revenue over fiscal year 2023. By doing so, the company managed to generate a return of 1,240% between its IPO in February 2014 and the time of writing (December 2024). Good for a return of a cool 27% annualized, over a period of more than 10 years. Not bad…

For non-production type of companies, for example in the software and consulting sectors, the limiting factor on growth is often its capability to find and recruit enough good employees. As such, the highest cost might be recruiting. Buying smaller competitors could be a cost-effective solution to add scale in a relatively cost-efficient way. On the condition that they can keep most employees of the

---

[23] At the time of writing, the 2024 annual report was not yet published, hence the slightly dated information.

target company happy. If everyone runs away shortly after the announcement of the deal, the entire point of the acquisition failed…

Acquisition of larger companies are often more difficult. The ego of senior managers often increases with the size of the company, making the process of acquiring and integrating larger companies more difficult. The corporate culture is also often more rusted in place: larger companies have more guidelines and policies, and it can be a shock to employees if they see all their "acquired rights" change or disappear. On the other hand, holding on to privileges for employees of the bought companies might make your current employees unhappy, as they are treated differently (or worse: worse!) compared to the newcomers. And corporate politics in all (and especially mid-level) managers might sicken the organization. Furthermore, larger acquisition and integration times lead to extended periods of uncertainty, during which the best employees are often targeted and hired away by recruiters or competitors while expensive underperformers often stay glued to their seats.

> **Small is Beautiful**
>
> This is also a reason why investing in small- and midcaps can be a sweet spot for value investors: there are plenty of opportunities for both organic growth and bolt-on acquisitions, while the total company is yet small enough so that the acquisitions can move the needle. In mega caps, smaller acquisitions don't move the needle anymore, and larger acquisitions run the risk of regulatory challenges (antitrust authorities), as well as clashes in the culture between both companies.

To summarize:

- ▸ Organic growth is preferred, as long as the potential of current factories and equipment are not yet fully utilized.
- ▸ Smaller bolt-on acquisitions are a very good way to speed up the growth profile of the company and help to consolidate the market. But don't forget to keep an eye on price paid, and on debt levels.

- Avoid companies that make large transformational acquisitions. Egos, corporate politics and integration expenses often harm the company more than originally anticipated.

Vertical Acquisitions

Vertical acquisitions are when you buy a (b2b) customer or supplier. The main advantage is that the company decreases its dependency from a third party. For example, an OEM buying its distributor, and thereby having more control over the selling process, marketing material, et cetera. And the other way around, by buying a parts supplier, there is more control on the quality of the products.

There are, however, also a number of drawbacks, which all too often outnumber the positives.

- Often a company further up or down the chain does more business than with your company alone. And its competitors will know that they are now owned by you, and therefore they might be less willing to do business. E.g. if we go back to the "OEM buys distributor" example, other OEMs won't like that you have real-time access to all their sales figures and promotions and might choose other distributors for their products, which means the company you acquired loses revenue and earnings, just because of your ownership.
- Synergies are often rather limited: the skills needed by a supplier or a client are different from the skills you need or have. In horizontal acquisitions, often lessons can be learned from each other. In vertical acquisitions, the overlap is a lot lower, so this is far less the case.
- And a last reason, which shouldn't really be taken into account by the management but which we are going to list anyway, just because we can as an analyst-author: it complicates the analysis of the performance of the company. E.g. the distributing business might be a lot more capital intensive (flooring space is needed, as is inventory, etc.) than the manufacturing business. So after the merger, the (headline) financial statements can become a mix of a capital intensive and a capital light business.

And depending on which segment of the total company was growing more, it will look as if the company became more efficient or less efficient in using its assets, just because the asset light business was growing faster or slower compared to the other part of the company. Which means investors might arrive at wrong conclusions...

Again, and obviously, management shouldn't really take this into account. And provide sufficient "segment information" on the separate business units for analysts to be able to do their job. (And for us, it might even imply improved opportunities: if other analysts don't do their homework, and just look at headline figures to arrive at conclusions, it could lead to stronger mispricing of the stock, thus giving the few that do put in the effort more rewarding returns on the long run...)

So for most businesses, horizontal acquisitions are to be preferred, with two notable exceptions.

The first is if a company is very reliant on one supplier, which implies this supplier has all the leverage over you: they can raise prices, they can drop the quality, and you would still be a client. Furthermore, in such a case it would be a disaster if that company were to be bought up by a competitor. In those cases, a vertical acquisition can be a good choice. For *strategic purposes*, that is, rather than for reasons of improving your growth profile or profitability.

The second exception is in the pharmaceutical industry. Big pharma often buys up biotech companies once their products get FDA approval, or when they reach late-stage trials with an approval expected sooner rather than later. Which often makes sense for both companies, because the nature of the business changes dramatically at that point: a small biotech company is mainly focused on research activities, whereas big pharma has more knowledge, experience and capabilities related to production, distribution and marketing of those products. So an acquisition at the right time might be a win-win for all players involved.

Acquisitions of unrelated companies

In order to be successful in acquiring companies, the acquisition should be in the circle of competences of the acquirer. It doesn't take a rocket scientist to understand this. But all too often, acquisitions happen for all the wrong reasons.

If *diversification* is stated as one of the most important reasons for the acquisition, then more often than not, shareholders will end up in tears because the acquirer is not the best owner for the acquired business and because synergies are very limited in those cases. This makes it very unlikely that the acquirer can genuinely offer the best price for the target company and still turn it into a profitable investment. Diversification should happen at the level of the investor (Yes, that means you!), not at the company level.

Most diversified holdings and conglomerates are valued at a discount compared to the sum of the parts. Which means value is created when they decide to split up in part, and destroy value when they acquire additional unrelated businesses to add to the collection. *"Diworsification"* is to be avoided...

A discussion about debt

It was stated before that bolt-on acquisitions are best. And that debt then follows a sawtooth-profile. The remark was also made that a company shouldn't overleverage itself: debt should remain manageable. In this section, one dives deeper into this topic.

Avoid companies with too much debt

Debt puts leverage on the equity returns of a company, and for a company generating healthy profits, a little leverage is often a good idea. However, companies that are too indebted are to be avoided. Because the lever also works in the opposite direction. And the opposite of a lever is a pincer. This might hurt one badly: give a healthy company too much debt and a couple of unpredicted setbacks, and soon the interest charges become larger than the earnings generated by the company, and hit you in the back. A situation that can turn the life of the equity investor look like the name of a rating agency: standard & poor.

// M&A, GROWTH, AND CAPITAL ALLOCATION

A difficulty when comparing reported debt numbers of companies is that everyone uses his own definition, which makes those numbers incomparable. So when analyzing a company, make sure to analyze the balance sheet carefully. When calculating the debt, count all interest-bearing liabilities, also the implicit ones. Leasing of assets that are needed to conduct the business are to be included as debt. Unfunded pension liabilities are a form of debt too.

> **Lease or buy?**
>
> Endless discussions happened in the past on whether a company should lease or buy its equipment, and whether the value of a company that leases should be the same or different from an identical company that bought its equipment. Luckily, since IFRS16 was introduced in 2019 as an accounting standard, financial leases are explicitly taken up as a liability in the balance sheet. Which created a bit more consensus on this topic. (The savvy analyst already made these adjustments prior to that date, based on information found in the notes to the financial statements.)
>
> The reason a lease should be counted as debt is that, for an equity holder, there is no difference whether the company
>
> - signed a binding lease agreement, which puts the company on the hook for monthly lease payments for the next couple of years.
> - Or signed a bank loan to finance the equipment, which puts the company on the hook to pay interests and installments over the next couple of years.
>
> Furthermore, as an equity holder, you are "last in line" in case of a bankruptcy. So also in case of a liquidation, there is no difference in the expected value one can receive.[24]

---

[24] From the equity-holders point of view, that is. For debtholders, there is a difference: the lessor, the leasing company that is, often remains the legal owner of the equipment and can recover ownership of the equipment if the lessee fails to make its lease payments. And is thus 'senior' to other debtholders like banks. But all of them get priority on the shareholder, so from a shareholders' perspective, there is no difference between a lease or a buy decision.

Note that for the management of a company, it can make a difference:

- Terms on leases can sometimes be more favorable because of the strong "collateral" held by the lessor. And because the lessor has a good knowledge of the value of the assets. (This is less often the case with banks, and their knowledge of the value of the collateral one offers. So they ask higher rates because their perceived risk is higher.)

- Leasing companies are sometimes more flexible in their terms because they have lots of clients looking for this type of equipment, so they can move equipment more easily from one client to the next, instead of having to sell it off like a bank would have to do.

So from a manager's point of view, the "lease versus buy" decision can still be a hard nut to crack. But as a financial analyst, the equipment used in the company should be accounted for as an asset, and the way it is financed as a liability. Clear and simple.

Next to the total level of debt, also the debt profile is to be assessed: A well-managed company has its debt maturities spread out over a somewhat longer time horizon. Avoid companies that have an overly large amounts of debt maturing at one point in time in the near future. Also avoid companies which have lots of debt maturing over the next one or two years, without a clear path on how to repay or refinance that debt. You never know what will happen, and the next credit crunch is only one pandemic, housing crisis, oil crisis or war away. If for whatever reason the company is not able to refinance its debt, huge losses are to be expected for the equity holders. Regardless of whether the reason for this is to be attributed to the company itself (e.g. difficulties at the company level) or not (e.g. a worldwide pandemic). So better safe than sorry…

It also tells you something about the risk profile of the CFO. Why should unnecessary risk be taken with the debt maturity profile? It's not like the company has a lot to gain by doing so. So why not be prudent?

// M&A, GROWTH, AND CAPITAL ALLOCATION

Also avoid companies with too much cash

Too much debt can be detrimental for the future of your company. However, there are also tons of companies with no debt at all who, on the contrary, hold a lot of cash on the balance sheet. This can be problematic too! Not because it can fail your company. But because it is detrimental for the returns generated on your investment: if half of the balance sheet is cash, generating no returns at all (or, at best, a couple of percentages on interest), then this basically halves the RoE of the company you buy. Because half of your investment's worth is just sitting as cash in the company, without doing anything with it...

Having an abundance of cash on the balance sheet can lead to complacency in management—the exact opposite of what happens in a management buyout (MBO) or leveraged buyout (LBO). In these scenarios, the operating company is typically burdened with significant debt, forcing management to scrutinize every expense and eliminate inefficiencies to ensure debt repayment. While this can drive exceptional operational efficiency, it also comes with a major downside: even an unforeseen setback beyond the company's control can trigger a dangerous debt spiral.

Conversely, when a company holds excessive cash reserves, cost-cutting measures tend to be less aggressive than they would be under financial pressure. Just as having extra personal savings can make an individual more relaxed about spending, an overly conservative balance sheet can lead to managerial complacency, resulting in suboptimal business decisions.

Next to this, it could also be an indication that management doesn't want to lose control over the money. This is money that actually belongs to shareholders and should be handed back to them. And it increases the risk that management will start feeling the need to spend the money on costly acquisitions or pet projects. Investments in such companies are to be avoided. (An exception is if you can take control of the company, or force management changes.)

To be clear, this is the case for companies where large amounts of cash on the balance sheet are a chronic situation. It can be perfectly rational for a company to sell a division and hold that cash for a couple of months because it eyes a specific acquisition itself, or because of planned buybacks or (extraordinary) dividends are planned in the foreseeable future. But if that cash remains on the balance sheet for years on end, then ask yourself questions with regard to the quality of the management, and with regard to your investment in the equity of this company.

> **How not to manage the balance sheet: the example of Van de Velde:**
>
> Van de Velde is a Belgian lingerie-maker. Contrary to its annual reports—a true eye-candy, with many pictures of the *product*—its financial statements look less appealing.
>
> A whopping 20% to 30% of the balance sheet is cash. And the company has no debt outstanding, besides a very small amount of leases and pension liabilities.
>
> | Van de Velde | 2019 | 2020 | 2021 | 2022 | 2023 |
> |---|---|---|---|---|---|
> | Cash and cash equivalents | 41,433 | 49,778 | 73,546 | 59,524 | 60,595 |
> | Inventories | 36,946 | 39,350 | 43,205 | 54,158 | 45,950 |
> | Trade receivables | 15,498 | 10,665 | 13,258 | 14,347 | 13,973 |
> | Other current assets | 10,875 | 5,312 | 3,878 | 8,354 | 6,029 |
> | **Total current assets** | **104,752** | **105,105** | **133,887** | **136,383** | **126,547** |
> | Goodwill | 4,546 | 4,546 | 4,617 | 4,529 | 4,558 |
> | Intangible assets | 23,940 | 22,409 | 20,276 | 20,575 | 20,415 |
> | Tangible fixed assets | 29,111 | 24,821 | 22,997 | 23,631 | 29,902 |
> | Right-of-use assets | 22,560 | 14,710 | 10,240 | 8,153 | 9,519 |
> | Participations | 11,631 | 12,525 | 13,744 | 13,556 | 10,646 |
> | Deferred tax assets | - | - | 227 | 227 | 199 |
> | Other fixed assets | 1,204 | 1,163 | 1,189 | 1,381 | 1,185 |
> | **Total assets** | **197,744** | **185,279** | **207,177** | **208,435** | **202,971** |
> | Trade and other payables | 21,508 | 18,429 | 25,365 | 25,594 | 21,911 |
> | Lease liabilities | 5,073 | 4,342 | 3,776 | 3,350 | 2,952 |
> | Income tax payable | 2,533 | 325 | 1,571 | 1,404 | 1,340 |
> | Other current liabilities | 3,004 | 1,170 | 1,676 | 1,763 | 1,682 |
> | **Total current liabilities** | **32,118** | **24,266** | **32,388** | **32,111** | **27,885** |
> | Provisions | 411 | 156 | 463 | 239 | 204 |
> | Provisions for lease liablities | 785 | 662 | 528 | 572 | 734 |
> | Pensions | 1,612 | 2,249 | 1,260 | 1,280 | 1,431 |
> | Lease liabilies | 17,480 | 12,229 | 8,425 | 5,549 | 6,675 |
> | Deferred tax liabilities | 465 | 701 | 707 | 368 | - |
> | Other non-current liabilities | 662 | - | - | - | - |
> | **Total liabilities** | **53,533** | **40,263** | **43,771** | **40,119** | **36,929** |
> | Grants | 380 | 366 | 285 | 203 | 122 |
> | Shareholders equity | 143,831 | 144,650 | 163,121 | 168,113 | 165,920 |
> | Total liabilities and shareholders' equity | 197,744 | 185,279 | 207,177 | 208,435 | 202,971 |

If you know that over 60% of the company is owned by the founder's family, it is easy to see that the majority shareholder could have easily taken the company private: lend money to buy out the minority shareholders, push the debt down to the operating company, and let the company pay off its debt. It would have made the family wealthier and allowed them to operate more discreetly (with fewer publication requirements).

Another opportunity would have been to pay out a large dividend, which can be invested by shareholders in other value-creating endeavors instead of just sitting there on the balance sheet, generating zero returns.

However, the majority-owner is very risk-averse, and as a result the company operates with a *conservative* or sub-optimal capital structure, which implies lower profitability on a higher invested capital amount. So instead of being a cash cow, an equity investment generated all moo and very little milk for its shareholders.

Share Buybacks versus Dividends

A company that generates cash but doesn't find enough growth opportunities can opt to buy back its own share or pay out a dividend. In both cases money flows towards its shareholders, but stock buybacks are (in most jurisdictions) more tax-efficient than dividends. So in most instances the former should be the preferred choice.

Share buybacks can be seen as "acquiring your own company." This can be the best allocation of capital, especially if you are operating in a mature sector. Organic growth might be impossible or sub-optimal,[25] and acquisitions may be blocked by antitrust authorities. But by buying back your own shares, the number of outstanding shares decreases. Which means next year's company earnings need to be divided over fewer outstanding shares, or thus the earnings per share increase. Which is exactly what one attempts to attain by growing organically or inorganically.

---

[25] Trying to gain market share in a mature market with an oligopoly structure might lead to a price war with your competitors, leaving every shareholder worse off...

Show me the money.

For example, oil companies, utilities, or telecom companies are types of companies that are often not really growing a lot. But they make a decent profit and pay out cash to shareholders. Nothing wrong with this from a company owner's perspective.

For this type of company it is of utmost importance to keep an eye on management, and specifically on their capital allocation decisions, though! The best thing they can do is generate buckets of cash, and let it flow through to the shareholders. But as a manager, it can be unbelievably tempting to make silly acquisitions in fintechs, start-ups or other unrelated businesses instead.

Taxes

Taxes on **dividends** vary a lot from country to country. Taxes in the United States are often 15% to 20%, depending on taxable income and filing status. In most European countries dividend tax are often even higher, and are in the 25% - 35% range. And often the money is even taxed twice: once in the country where the company is incorporated, and a second time in the shareholders' own tax jurisdiction, leading to even higher rates.

If the tax rate paid adds up to a high percentage, then companies that pay out a large percentage of their profits are to be avoided. The opposite can be true if you happen to live in a low-taxed country, or if your investments are structured in a fiscally efficient way. If you have a comparative tax advantage compared to "the market," high-dividend stocks are to be sought after!

On **share buybacks**, there are often no taxes, or very small taxes. In the US, the Biden administration imposed a 1% tax on share buybacks. In Europe, often no taxes are to be paid on share buybacks, which should make this the preferred way of returning capital to shareholders.

Signal function of the dividend

Often, twisted justifications are made in favor of paying dividends, despite their inefficiencies.

One of the most frequently cited arguments is that dividends serve as a **"signal"** to the market—a sign of confidence from management about the company's future prospects. The reasoning goes that executives are reluctant to cut dividends once established, so any substantial increase is a strong indication that management believes the company can sustain a higher profitability, and the higher payout, even in tougher economic conditions.

While this logic holds some truth, it often causes more harm than good. For one, it may pressure companies to **maintain dividends during economic downturns**, stubbornly paying out precious cash even when it would be far wiser to retain those funds for operational stability or strategic investments. On the flip side, in times of prosperity, this signaling pressure may lead management to **hoard excessive cash**, prioritizing a steady dividend over more productive uses of capital. The result? A suboptimal allocation of resources, where capital that could have been used for expansion, innovation, or share buybacks instead sits idly on the balance sheet. Like a miser stuffing money under a mattress to avoid the discomfort of an uncertain future.

Another common but flawed argument is that dividends provide shareholders—particularly retirees—with a **steady income stream** to live off. While this may seem intuitive, it is, in reality, a **cognitive fallacy**. A dividend payment does not increase a shareholder's net worth; it merely transfers money from the company's account to the shareholders, minus a toll paid to the tax collector along the way. It's akin to taking a few bills from your left pocket, moving them to your right pocket, and being charged a fee for the privilege. A more tax-efficient alternative? **Share buybacks.** If an investor requires income, they can sell a small portion of their holdings when needed, effectively creating their own dividend without forcing the entire shareholder base into a taxable event.

In short, the ideal company is one that earns high returns on capital and reinvests it all. Buybacks are the second-best option. Dividends only come in third place on the preference list: it is better than hoarding cash in the company, but unnecessary handouts to Uncle Sam should be avoided whenever possible.

Chapter Summary

- Buy growing companies. The entire economy is built on growth. Shrinking is expensive. Cheap-looking companies in a shrinking market are often a *value trap*, and to be avoided at all costs.
- Smaller bolt-on acquisitions can be as good as growing organically and are the capital allocation of choice as an investor. Look for companies following such a strategy. One way to recognize them, is by looking for a sawtooth-profile when plotting debt levels over time.
- Larger transformational transactions can be good as well, but carry a higher risk. Often management is too optimistic in estimating synergies, and the integration of large companies can be more difficult. Consider whether it is worth temporarily exiting the stock, if your estimation of the intrinsic value is relatively close to the current market value (meaning there is no large margin of safety).
- Vertical acquisitions have lower synergies and often complicate the financial analysis going forward. This is only a good use of money if your company is very reliant on that supplier or customer. (But if this is the case, why did you buy the company in the first place?) The pharmaceutical sector is a notable exception here.
- *Diworsification* is to be avoided. Conglomerates deserve a discount.
- Companies should have a decent level of debt. Too much debt may lead to underinvestment, jeopardizing the future of the company. Too little debt (or a net cash position) makes life too easy for a company, and results in the avoidance of cost-cutting exercises. And thus in suboptimal management of the company. It might also lead to pet projects.
- Share buybacks are to be preferred over dividends, given its tax treatment in most jurisdictions.
- If you happen to live in a low-tax region, this gives you a comparative advantage to other investors, and you may profit from actively searching for high dividend payers.

CHAPTER 7

Quality of the business

> *"The best businesses make money while you sleep; the worst ones keep you up at night wondering where your money went."*
>
> - UNKNOWN

In Chapter 4, a number of characteristics of what a great company looks like were already explained: the business model should be like a moat, or like an unregulated toll bridge. But how to recognize these high-quality businesses? There are literally thousands of companies listed on the exchange, and only a minority of them are actual great businesses. And nobody has sufficient time to go through each and every one of them and get a good grasp of what the business is actually doing, and make a thorough assessment of what the quality of each and every business is like.

In this chapter, the focus is on what the financial figures of high-quality companies look like. Thus, one can quickly browse through the historical numbers to see whether or not the company is indeed performing like a high-quality business. The better these characteristics are, the higher the likelihood that the business is indeed great. This framework can be used to quickly filter and narrow down a long list of potential investments as "worth investigating" or "not worth my time and efforts." Obviously, this is only a starting point.

Next, the business needs to be understood from a more fundamental point of view, as opposed to just its historical financial statements. To be able to make an educated guess that, one, the numbers were not a fluke or a coincidence. And two, that the probability that the company and its business model will not be under attack in the near future either, and will thus (most likely) continue performing the way it does in the near future, as it did in the recent past.

And afterwards, once one is confident that the company under investigation is indeed a great business, the stock price enters the equation. Because even for great

// QUALITY OF THE BUSINESS

businesses it is possible to overpay. If the price is not right, you shouldn't buy the stock, even if the business is great. For those companies, it might still be a good idea to keep them on a "*watch list*" with a target price at which you are willing to reconsider. And be ready to reinvestigate a potential buy decision once the market offers you the stock at the right price, e.g. during a market crash or during periods of higher stock market volatility...

So, what are the qualities to look for in the financials of a company?

Steadiness of Revenue and Earnings

When analyzing the income statement of the company, there are two basic qualities one likes to see: steadiness and leverage.

When given the choice between a company with highly volatile earnings and one with a more stable and predictable profitability pattern, steadiness is to be favored. Consistent revenue and operating earnings are a strong indication that the company is less vulnerable to economic downturns, possesses the ability to pass on price increases when faced with inflation, or benefits from long-term contracts that provide greater visibility into future revenue. This stability not only makes financial forecasting more reliable but also reduces uncertainty for investors. Therefore, it is often better to have a company growing every year by 8%, than to have a company that grows 20% one year, and shrinks 3% the next year[26].

The greater the confidence in a company's future performance, the lower the perceived risk of the investment. And in the world of investing, lower risk often justifies a higher valuation. As a result, companies with steady earnings patterns typically deserve a slightly higher earnings multiple, reflecting the premium investors are willing to pay for predictability and resilience in an unpredictable market.

For example, the income stream to The Coca-Cola Company (TCCC) has a high degree of predictability. The sales of sugary water is a little weather-dependent, but is not going to double or halve from one year to the next. And if prices of sugar, packaging material or transport increase, TCCC will adjust its prices, and

---

[26] Although both end up growing a little over 16% over a 2-year period.

the majority of the customers are still going to pay the increased price to get their favorite drink.

> ### "Habit" products
>
> One of the reasons the sales volumes of The Coca-Cola Company are relatively stable is also that it is a consumer staples product, that is bought (in supermarkets) or ordered (in bars and restaurants) on a very regular basis. Thus, it has become a certain habit for a lot of customers. This also means that not every customer is going to check the price of the product every time they order or purchase a Coke. As a result, customers are going to keep buying the product and might not even notice occasional small price increases (to a certain extent).
>
> A second element is that it is relatively cheap. When buying a new laptop, customers are going to compare prices and thus compare brands and models for every purchase. For Coke, this is not necessarily the case. And in general, for relatively cheap products, customers are going to be a bit more loyal to the brand.
>
> In general, the cheaper a product and the more frequently a product is bought, the more loyal the customer base is going to be. This indicates a higher-quality business, which is reflected in more stable growth in the financial statements from one year to the next.

Still, one always needs to be on the lookout for changes in market circumstances. E.g. a large disruption in the market might occasionally occur and could shake up even sectors that were historically very resilient. AI could shake-up the B2B market for outsourced call centers, leading to depressed stock prices for companies providing such services.

The easiest way to check the consistency of the revenue growth and/or earnings growth, is to calculate the R-squared of the last couple of years. In the graph below, the revenues of Microsoft and ExxonMobil are charted, over the last 10 years.

// QUALITY OF THE BUSINESS

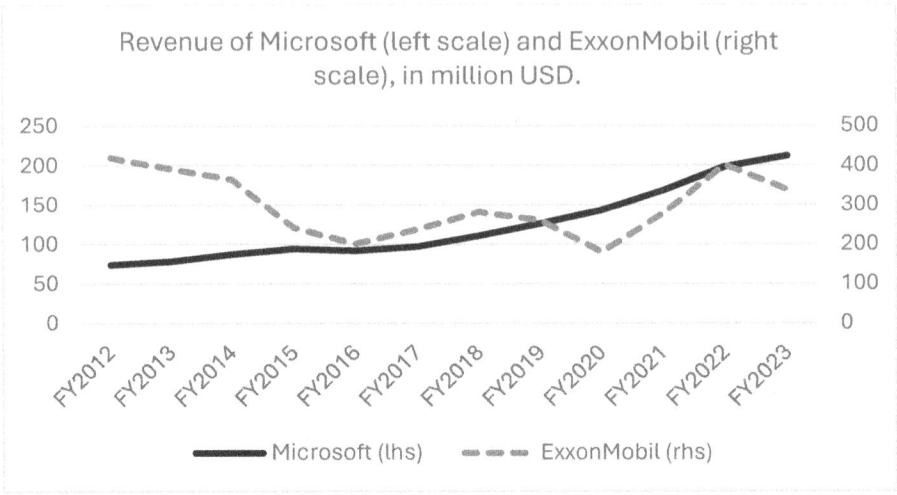

As one can see, the revenue of Microsoft is extremely consistent over time. The R-squared of the revenue equals 89% over this period. On the other hand, ExxonMobil has a more volatile revenue pattern, with an R-squared of only 5%. It would lead us too far to discuss all the reasons behind this, but locked-in and subscription-based revenues and the high switching costs (if at all possible to switch to a different software provider) give Microsoft extreme pricing power and very predictable revenue streams. ExxonMobil on the other hand is a commodity player, hence it has no pricing power, so its sales prices (and revenue) are strongly dependent on the oil prices of the market, which are largely outside the control of the company. Thus, based on this quick analysis, Microsoft is the better business, and would be the preferred company to buy stocks from... **if they were trading at the same multiple of through-the-cycle earnings or EBIT**! Obviously, we are not the only ones making this observation, and thus Microsoft trades at 36x earnings while ExxonMobil trades at 13x earnings. So which one is the better buy, given the graph above and the stated prices?

The correct answer is: we are looking at too limited information to determine which company is the better buy given the price differential. A lot more analysis is required, taking into account the balance sheet, future prospects, et cetera. One shouldn't come to a conclusion to buy or sell a stock based on one graph. But this discussion should at least give some insight and uncover just another piece of the puzzle of the intelligent investor.

As with everything in equity analysis, this rule is not carved in stone. If a company made a large acquisition, the "bought revenue" will cause a jump in the number, thereby distorting the R-squared[27]. And while the integration of acquisitions is always a bit of a risk, this is not what one wants to measure or penalize with this metric. So also here, results are to be interpreted with caution, and with the knowledge of the drivers behind the numbers...

Leverage

A second quality to be on the lookout for is (both financial and operational) leverage. Simply said, it means that the lower one gets on the income statement, the higher the percentage increase of the number should be. For example, a 3% increase in revenue translates in a 5% increase in gross profit, an 8% increase in operating profit, and a 12% increase in net profit. And if the company bought back some shares, this might even lead to a 13% increase in earnings per share.

This was already touched upon in Chapter 4, but let's dissect this example a little further. The first part—the increase in gross profit exceeding the revenue growth—is based on operational leverage, which refers to how certain costs do not scale linearly with revenue growth, hence amplifying the impact of changes in sales on a company's profitability.

Businesses with high fixed costs (like factories, equipment, or software development) see profits grow faster than revenue once they pass their break-even point, because their costs don't rise as quickly as output. To make the example concrete, imagine a cylindrical barrel, oven, or whatever you need in a production process. The inside of the barrel holds your product, the outside shell is made of steel. The volume the cylinder can hold is calculated as $\pi r^2 h$. The surface area is calculated as $2\pi rh + 2\pi r^2$. If the barrel gets bigger, the volume increases much faster than the surface area. This implies economies of scale: less steel is needed per unit of content to be stored. Or less heat is lost when needing to melt a certain volume, et cetera. This might sound simple, but the truth is that many production processes

---

[27] With more regular 'bolt-on acquisitions', the R-squared will be less distorted than by one large transformational deal. And the former is preferred above the latter. So even with acquisitions, the metric somewhat holds. Although if there is are large deltas in sales from year to year, we prefer it to be attributable to acquisitions or divestitures, rather than extreme cyclicality of the market the company operates in.

// QUALITY OF THE BUSINESS

show this kind of scaling throughout production facilities. We're not even talking yet about improved cost-efficiencies if the same production line can run at higher versus lower utilization rates.

Moving on to the second part: "a 5% increase in gross profit should lead to an 8% increase in operating profit." While the exact numbers of the example are hypothetical, operating profit should grow faster than gross profit. Because a few costs are fixed: you don't need more CEOs, financial reporting, legal and compliance if you sell a bit more product. Those costs are (more or less) fixed. And the more units a company produces, the more product these costs can be "spread out" over, leading to higher profit margins.

Financial debt also puts a lever on profits: interest charges are a percentage paid on debt outstanding, and thus not correlated to the operating profit. Imagine a company generating 1 million USD in operating profit (= EBIT, Earnings Before Interest and Taxes), and assume a 25% tax rate. If the company has no debt, there is no interest expense. So the net profit after tax equals 750,000 USD. If the company had 5 million USD of debt outstanding at a 10% interest rate, 500,000 USD interest would have to be paid. So the net profit becomes (1,000,000 − 500,000)*(1-0.25) = 375,000 USD. Now, if in the next year the company grows EBIT by 10% to 1,1 million USD, then in the debt-free example the company posts net profits after tax of 825,000 USD, an increase of 10% versus the original 750k net profit of the prior year, and an equal percentage increase as the EBIT increased. But in the debt-example, the net profit becomes (1,100,000 − 500,000)*(1-0.25) = 450,000 USD. This is an increase of 20% versus the 375k profit of the prior year. Because the debt charges are "fixed," they don't increase with the increase in EBIT numbers, and put a lever between the operating profit and the net profit, similar as fixed costs put a lever between the gross profit and the net profit.

All this to say: the lower one gets on the income statement, the higher the percentage increase of the numbers should be. A quality company should see steady revenue growth, which translates to more impressive growth in EBIT and net profit numbers. And very conveniently, screening tools can be designed to identify and highlight companies that exhibit this behavior.

DuPont Decomposition

This section takes a deeper look at the **Return on Equity (RoE)** ratio—a valuable metric for assessing a company's efficiency in generating returns relative to the equity invested in the business. RoE serves as a key indicator of how effectively a company utilizes shareholder capital to create profits.

However, its usefulness extends beyond a simple efficiency measure. RoE can be **decomposed into distinct components**, each offering deeper insights into the specific factors driving profitability. By breaking it down, analysts and company managers can better understand **how** a company achieves its returns, identify key performance drivers, and pinpoint areas for potential improvement. This breakdown not only enhances financial analysis but also helps guide strategic decisions aimed at optimizing profitability.

In what follows, a step-by-step explanation of the Dupont-analysis is given. Author's note: if you already know this concept, feel free to skip to the next chapter.

Let's begin with defining what the RoE is:

$$RoE = \frac{Net\ Income}{Shareholders'\ Equity}$$

As discussed earlier, this is a decent ratio to measure the performance and quality of a company. The higher, the better.

However, this ratio can be reformulated, and be written as follows:

$$RoE = \frac{Net\ Income}{Sales} * \frac{Sales}{Total\ Assets} * \frac{Total\ Assets}{Shareholders'\ Equity}$$

Now the ratio is decomposed in 3 terms:

- Net income over sales gives the net income margin. It measures how much profit the company makes for every dollar of revenue.
- Sales over total assets gives the asset turnover. And is a measure to determine how much assets a company needs in order to generate its revenue.
- Total assets over shareholders' equity gives the financial leverage of the company.

// QUALITY OF THE BUSINESS

Sales and total assets each appear both in the numerator and in the denominator, and can thus be deleted to arrive again at the original RoE formula. However, by rewriting it this way, it makes it very obvious that a company has three primary ways to improve its RoE profile:

1. **Increase profitability per unit sold** – By raising prices, reducing costs, or improving operational efficiency, a company can generate more profit for each product or service sold.
2. **Optimize asset efficiency** – Generating the same level of revenue while using fewer assets improves asset turnover, allowing the company to achieve higher returns with a leaner balance sheet.
3. **Leverage debt** – By taking on more debt, a company can amplify returns on equity since borrowed funds can be used to generate additional profits without requiring more shareholder investment.

However, leveraging debt comes with inherent risks and limitations. The more debt a company carries, the higher its **interest payments**, which can erode net income margins. At extreme levels, excessive debt can lead to financial distress or even bankruptcy. Therefore, while debt can enhance RoE, it must be used judiciously—too much leverage can turn a financial advantage into a dangerous liability.

One can even take the RoE decomposition one step further, and extend this formula from 3 to 5 factors:

$$RoE = \frac{Net\ Income}{Pre-Tax\ Income} * \frac{Pre-Tax\ Income}{EBIT} * \frac{EBIT}{Sales} * \frac{Sales}{Total\ Assets} * \frac{Total\ Assets}{Shareholders'\ Equity}$$

Each of these terms tells us something about the company.

- Net Income over pre-tax income gives us the tax burden.
- Pre-tax income over EBIT gives us the interest burden
- EBIT over Sales is the operating margin
- Sales over total assets gives us the asset turnover
- Total Assets / Shareholders' equity gives us the leverage ratio

The tax burden is often something that cannot be influenced too heavily. Of course a company can try to optimize its tax expenses as good as possible, and reinvestments often also lead to lower tax percentages.

The interest burden is something to keep an eye on, and one you don't want to see too stretched: if this ratio is too low, a small decrease in pre-tax income, or a hike in interest rates, can make the company loss-making, because the debt will keep biting. This ratio gives an indication on how much room there still is to stretch the balance sheet and take on more debt. But don't be too greedy on this one!

The operating margin, EBIT over sales, should be as high as possible. The better your market, and the better your brand and product, the more you can mark up your products. This gives an indication of how good the company truly is from an operational point of view.

The asset turnover and financial leverage ratio are similar as in the three-way decomposition.

Why Use DuPont Analysis?

- **To pinpoint the drivers of profitability**: By splitting ROE into these three components, you can see if profitability changes are due to changes in margins, asset efficiency, or the firm's capital structure.
- **To identify operational weaknesses**: For instance, a dropping ROE might be due to deteriorating asset turnover rather than reduced profit margins.
- **For benchmarking and trend analysis**: Comparing each component across time or between different companies can reveal trends or best practices that drive stronger ROE.

Let's illustrate this with an example used earlier, the DebtCo as used in chapter 5.

// QUALITY OF THE BUSINESS

Income Statement	Year 1	Year 2	Year 3	Year 4	Year 5
Sales	1,000	1,000	1,000	1,000	1,000
COGS	- 400	- 400	- 400	- 400	- 400
Gross profit	600	600	600	600	600
SG&A, excl D&A	- 200	- 200	- 200	- 200	- 200
R&D	- 175	- 175	- 175	- 175	- 175
EBITDA	225	225	225	225	225
Depreciation & Amortization	- 125	- 125	- 125	- 125	- 125
EBIT	100	100	100	100	100
Interest	- 30	- 30	- 30	- 30	- 30
EBT	70	70	70	70	70
Income tax	- 14	- 14	- 14	- 14	- 14
Net profit	56	56	56	56	56

Free Cash Flow Calculation	Year 1	Year 2	Year 3	Year 4	Year 5
Net profit	56	56	56	56	56
Depreciation & Amortization	125	125	125	125	125
CapEx	- 125	- 125	- 125	-125	- 125
FCF	56	56	56	56	56
Dividend paid out	- 56	- 56	- 56	- 56	- 56
Added to Retained Earnings	-	-	-	-	-

Simplified Balance Sheet	Year 0	Year 1	Year 2	Year 3	Year 4	Year 5
Cash	-	-	-	-	-	-
Productive Assets	1,000	1,000	1,000	1,000	1,000	1,000
Total Assets	1,000	1,000	1,000	1,000	1,000	1,000
Liabilities	600	600	600	600	600	600
Shareholders' Equity	400	400	400	400	400	400
Total Liabilities & Stockholders' Equity	1,000	1,000	1,000	1,000	1,000	1,000

The company generates a net profit of 56 USD, on 400 USD of shareholders' equity. Hence, the Return on Equity equals 14%.

However, this can be decomposed to:

- A net profit margin of 5.6% (56 net profit on 1,000 of sales)
- An asset turnover of 1.0: (1,000 sales on 1,000 of assets)
- A financial leverage of 2.5 (1,000 of assets on 400 of equity)

Which then translates to a RoE of $0.056 * 1 * 2.5 = 14\%$.

Notice that the example of EquityCo, in which the company was all equity financed, would lead to an RoE of 8%, based on:

- A net profit margin of 8.0%. The net profit is higher, because no interest charges are to be paid if the company is all equity financed.
- The asset turnover remains unchanged at 1.0.
- And the financial leverage becomes 1.0 as well, if the company is all equity financed: total equity equals total assets.

We refer to chapter 5 for the corresponding income statement and balance sheet for the example of EquityCo. But it is obvious that the RoE increased by adding some leverage, because the interest burden (and corresponding decrease in net profit) was more than offset by the increase in financial leverage.

// QUALITY OF THE BUSINESS

If we retake the leveraged example, DebtCo, and dive a little deeper. We get:

- An operating margin of 10% (100 EBIT on 1,000 of revenue)
- The asset turnover is 1.0
- The financial leverage is 2.5
- The interest burden equals 0.70 (= EBT of 70/ EBIT of 100)
- The tax burden equals 0.80 (= 56/70, or a 20% tax rate)

Once again the RoE is 14%, now decomposed as 0.10*1.0*2.5*0.70*0.80.

A decomposition like this can help assess where the value is coming from, and whether this performance is sustainable, will likely deteriorate, or can be improved in the future. Using the examples above, it is easy to see that adding a bit of leverage was useful: the levered example had a higher RoE because the financial leverage boosted returns more than the interest charges decreased net profits. At the same time, the interest charges were still manageable, with an interest burden of 0.70.

RoE decompositions are thus an elementary tool to assess the quality of a company and very useful for cross-company comparisons.

But at the same time, it is a useful tool to discover risks. For example, if EBT would only be a small fraction of EBIT, a small increase in interest rates or a small decrease in operating profit would mean the company could run into difficulties to cover its interest charges. And soon, the company could be working for its debtholders, instead of for its equity holders ... a situation that is to be avoided.

It is also a very useful tool to assess the evolution of returns over time. If the RoE increased or decreased from one year to the next, was it because of operating margins? Or because of financial engineering and changes in the capital structure? Or was it caused by external effects, like a lower tax rate or lower interest rates? And how likely is it that this trend will continue in the future?

Chapter Summary

- Great companies show a steady growth in financial figures. A company that grows 5% per year is better than one that grows 20% in one year and shrinks 15% in the next. Look for high R-squared figures on sales, gross profit and EBIT numbers.

- A great company has operational leverage: steady revenue growth translates into a higher percentage increase of EBIT. And a bit of financial leverage boosts net profit even further. So the lower one gets on the income statement, the higher the growth percentage becomes.

- A RoE decomposition will give valuable insights into the reasons why the return of a company is what it is. Be careful if all growth comes from financial leverage. Increases in operating margins and asset turnover is what one loves to see.

- Price always comes into the equation. Even the greatest business can be a lousy investment if one bought at too high a price.

CHAPTER 8

Quality of the Sector & Region

"If you want to be a millionaire, start with a billion dollars and launch a new airline"

- RICHARD BRANSON

In this chapter, we are going to dive into the qualities of sectors and regions. What to look for sector-wise? Are there sectors to be avoided? Should one invest worldwide, or focus on specific regions? And which regions to avoid?

Quality of the Sector

Just like the previous chapter, this section partly overlaps with chapter 4 as well: the qualities of a good sector are also reflected as qualities sought after in good companies. However, in this section the emphasis is put on the sector as a whole, instead of at the specific company level.

As mentioned earlier, **growth** is an important aspect of the entire economy. One wants to invest with tailwind, not headwind. Invest in companies who are active in growing sectors, not shrinking ones. Warren Buffett famously quipped, *"When a manager with a good reputation meets an industry with a bad reputation. It is normally the industry that leaves with its reputation intact"*.

It is still better to own a company that grows with 12%, thereby underperforms its sector that grows at 15%, than to own shares in a company that grows 4% in a sector that grows 2%. The latter management did an outstanding job, but the faster-growing one is the more financially rewarding one...

// QUALITY OF THE SECTOR & REGION

Preferably, the growth is also **steady**. A good sector is not that cyclical. Therefore, consider how the sector performed during recessions and economic downturns.

The sector should have **high barriers to entry**, keeping other entrepreneurs from entering the field. Branding, patents, permits, and people's habits are good barriers to entry. The requirement to invest high amounts of money is also a barrier to entry but is not favored: a **low capital intensity** is preferred, as it enables a company to grow faster, without needing to eat out of the shareholders' free cash flow.

Avoid sectors that survive because of subsidies and government grants. Companies in a good sector manage to earn healthy profit margins on their own, without needing an uncle Sam to support them.

Avoid sectors that run the risk of being disrupted by new technologies. This applies even if the companies in such sectors see the disruption coming and prepare themselves and invest in that new technology as well. Technological disruptions often first lead to a period of overinvesting and reduced profit margins, because everyone is trying to win (or protect) their market share. And once the fight is over, it is rarely the incumbent players that end up still being on top.

Also make sure to **keep an eye on geopolitics** and global trends. Trade wars can have nasty influences on certain sectors. Tariffs are the talk-of-the-day as long as Donald Trump resides in the White House, and they can impact the ebbs and flows of import and export.

Preferably, the sectors one invests in are also not too vulnerable to energy prices, or can promptly pass-through such costs without any delays.

And look for sectors that operate in an oligopoly. Three or four players dividing the market among themselves, with high barriers to entry for new players, is an ideal situation for shareholders. Avoid fragmented sectors with excessive competition and low pricing power.

A case for investing in local monopolies

Monopolies, where only one company can provide a good or service, often face a lot of scrutiny by antitrust authorities. And rightly so. Because such companies have the ultimate pricing power, and no incentive at all to innovate or to deliver good quality and good customer service, all customers remain customers having no alternative. They are a shareholder's dream—as long as antitrust authorities keep their hands off—but a client's nightmare. This is why regulators often intervene in these cases.

However, an interesting situation sometimes occurs for producers of relatively cheap but large (or heavy) products. One cannot transport bricks, insulation material, or glass bottles, for example, over long distances and still deliver the goods at a competitive price. Which can lead to "local monopolies": if one company owns all factories in a range of a couple of hundred miles, then this company basically has a "local monopoly" in that region. No one else can deliver the same products at attractive prices in that area, so the company can raise prices and generate excessive profit margins. All the while, if the market is more fragmented in a country-wide analysis, antitrust authorities are also less likely to intervene, which can provide excellent investment opportunities.

If such companies do bolt-on acquisitions in a smart way, they can keep growing, and increasing the area in which the local monopoly exists, to a sometimes surprisingly large extent before regulators limit further expansions. (And they seldomly break up an existing one...)

Prefer wealthy customers

When investing in companies, one often focuses on their production capabilities, market share, or brand reputation. Yet, an overlooked aspect of their success lies in the financial well-being and purchasing power of the customers they serve. In essence, it's challenging for a business to make substantial profits if its customers themselves operate on slim margins or struggle to stay afloat. Conversely, when a company's clients enjoy healthy profit margins, that prosperity can flow upward, allowing the supplier to command a higher price for its goods or services.

Consider a glass bottles and containers supplier like Verallia. Selling bottles to small, family-owned Italian wineries—charming though they may be—usually means razor-thin profit margins. These clients cannot afford to pay much more than the bare minimum for their inputs. On the other hand, if that same supplier provides bottles to global luxury brands like LVMH or Diageo, both known for high-end spirits and wines, the math changes. These clients, flush with the buying power of wealthy consumers, can absorb higher costs, enabling the supplier to earn more.

Likewise, a company staffing restaurants may find itself constantly squeezed by tight-lipped budgets and slender margins, but a firm that provides personal staff to a royal household or an ultra-wealthy patron stands in a different league. The ability and willingness of the customer to pay top dollars can translate directly into healthier margins for the supplier.

This principle often becomes most pronounced in the luxury sector. High-end goods and services cater to customers who have ample disposable income and are willing—if not eager—to spend lavishly on quality, exclusivity, and reputation. By targeting these affluent markets, businesses can achieve pricing power that would be impossible in more cost-sensitive customer segments.

As an investor, pay close attention to the nature of a company's clientele. Are they struggling just to keep the lights on, or are they flush with cash and seeking premium products or solutions? While this rule may not hold perfectly across all industries or scenarios, it provides a valuable lens through which to assess a company's potential profitability. The prosperity of the customer can, in a very tangible sense, become the prosperity of the firm. And by extension, the prosperity of the investor who owns its stock.

Capital intensity and cyclicality go hand in hand

Capital-intensive industries are, by their very nature, deeply intertwined with the economic cycle. Their defining characteristic—the need for substantial upfront investment in machinery, infrastructure, and technology—makes them highly sensitive to fluctuations in demand. Once these investments are made, they cannot easily be undone. Factories, power plants, and transportation networks cannot be scaled down overnight when market conditions shift. The burden of high fixed costs remains, even when revenues decline, forcing companies to weather downturns with limited flexibility.

The cyclical nature of these industries stems from their dependency on broader economic trends. When times are good, businesses and consumers spend more freely. Industrial production surges, real estate developments multiply, and airlines place orders for new fleets. But when recessions hit, demand dries up just as quickly. Consumers delay major purchases, companies put expansion plans on hold, and projects that once seemed essential are shelved indefinitely. The result is a painful contraction in industries that had, only months earlier, been thriving. Compounding this volatility is the fact that capital-intensive sectors often require years—sometimes decades—to see a return on investment. Decision-making in these industries is necessarily long-term. A company may break ground on a new factory during an economic boom, only to see it completed when demand is already in decline. The inability to quickly adjust to changing conditions means these industries often overinvest during good times, creating excess capacity that exacerbates downturns when demand falters.

Another key factor driving cyclicality is the reliance on external financing. Because capital-intensive businesses require large sums of money to fund expansion and maintain operations, they are highly dependent on the availability of credit. During economic booms, banks lend freely, interest rates remain low, and funding for new projects flows easily. In contrast, when recessions take hold, credit tightens, borrowing becomes expensive, and many companies struggle to finance ongoing operations, let alone new investments.

Ultimately, capital-intensive sectors are cyclical because their very structure leaves them exposed to the highs and lows of economic activity. Their long lead times, reliance on credit, and susceptibility to demand swings make them prone to overexpansion in good times and painful contractions in bad. It is a pattern that repeats itself decade after decade—booms that fuel excessive investment, followed by downturns that force a painful reckoning.

// QUALITY OF THE SECTOR & REGION

When capital and cyclicality meet: The example of Mohawk

Mohawk is a producer of flooring and ceramic products. They are the worldwide market leader, but this market is extremely fragmented, as illustrated by their 2% market share, which is indeed sufficient to be the market leader...

This sector has two important characteristics: the fixed costs for production equipment are high. And production is cheaper if larger batches of product are produced, because adjusting the machinery to produce a different type of floor takes time.

As a result, there is a natural drive for overproduction. Margins can easily be increased by running larger batches and storing the excess in inventory for a while. This causes trouble as soon as an economic downturn hits: as soon as demand drops, everybody has excess inventory. The logical solution for companies with too much inventory is to decrease production, until the inventory levels drop to more normal levels. But in the flooring industry, decreasing production levels means higher average production costs. And at a time of economic hardship, companies want to avoid this. (Often, the management is still optimistic and in denial about the oncoming economic downturn. "Next week orders will be better. Keep producing!") So they opt for another solution: temporarily dropping prices or giving additional promotions.

But the thing is, demand for flooring is not super elastic: it is not because flooring drops in prices that everyone is going to replace their floor. On the contrary, in economic downturns, building and remodeling are often postponed, because lending becomes more difficult. So demand does not recover. And inventory keeps growing.

All companies also have the incentive to keep producing as long as their selling prices cover the variable production costs: the fixed assets are already paid for anyway. So, selling prices keep on dropping until a number of companies go broke, or until the economy recovers.

The opposite is also true: in good times, everyone earns very good money. Because all production lines run at full capacity (whing implies low

> production costs), and if demand exceeds supply, no promotions need to be given, and prices can even be hiked: there appears to be pricing power. And this situation can continue for quite a while, because increasing capacity requires large investments, and building additional production lines takes a lot of time. Usually, by the time they are ready, the good times are over and the problem of excess capacity is exacerbated. And the illusion of pricing power vanishes into thin air[28].

Quality of the Region

How to define the regions

With regards to the regions to invest in, it is important to first define what is understood as the region.

In this book, with region, we mean the location where business is done. It includes the places where employees are working, the places where production takes place, and the places where products are sold. While this might sound trivial, investors sometimes confuse this with the region where the stock is trading. And all too often, pie charts of investment funds show regional exposure based on either where the headquarters of a company are, or where a company is listed rather than where the actual employees are based, and where the goods are produced or sold.

E.g. Novartis is based in Switzerland and trades on the Swiss stock exchange. But the company sells pharmaceutical products worldwide. So this gives the investor worldwide exposure. Its exposure to the Swiss economy is actually rather limited...

E.g. Prosus is a Dutch holding company. But its main investments are Tencent (Chinese app and gaming studio), Meituan (Chinese shopping platform) and Swiggy (Indian food delivery company). Which means an investment in Prosus is mainly an investment in China and India, not in the Netherlands.

---

[28] Yours truly learned this lesson the hard way. Especially during times of economic expansion, it can be surprisingly hard to distinguish between true pricing power, and temporary pricing power due to market shortages – that will be resolved sooner rather than later. Stay alert for these situations, and avoid getting *floored...*

// QUALITY OF THE SECTOR & REGION

What qualities to look for in a region

The most important aspect of a country or region is that the area is **open for business**. The more business-friendly the rules, regulations and political direction is going in, the better for equity investors.

One aspect of it is **low taxes**: the life of a company is a zero-sum game against the taxman. Every dollar spent on taxes doesn't go into the pocket of the investor, and vice versa. So corporate taxes, and their direction, are an important consideration.

For example, in the United States corporate taxes were lowered on 1 January 2018, from 35% to 21%. This was a huge windfall for all investors. The way to look at it is as follows: in 2017 the US Government is an economic owner of 35% of every business. And all other shareholders combined only get assigned 65% of the pre-tax profit generated by their "fully owned" company. From 2018 onward, the tax code changes, and now all of a sudden those same shareholders get assigned 79% of the pre-tax profits. Which implies every stock is now worth 21.5% more (79/65-1) than before the tax change was put on the table[29].

At least equally important as low taxes are **business-friendly regulations**. Once again, the United States scores quite well: it is relatively easy to do business, and the amount of red tape is still manageable compared to many other regions. India is a notable example of a region that *perfected* its red tape. A country with 1.4 billion potential customers would normally be very interesting to do business in, but its excessive red tape makes it extremely hard to build and grow a company in that region. And lots of shareholder value has vanished because of it.

As an example, to be active in the Indian food business, a company requires three different kinds of licenses: one from the central government, one state license, and one basic license. Each of them requires a number of different forms and supporting documentation to be submitted to and approved by various departments. A "Food Safety and Standards Authority of India" license requires eight different forms to be submitted. The state-level version requires 14. And for the central one, 16 different forms are needed. Also, obtaining these licenses takes more than 60 days for most of them. Not a very efficient system to establish, manage and grow a business in.

---

[29] Assuming the lower tax rate remains in place until eternity, that is.

Another important aspect is the ability to resize companies. Costs are like fingernails: they need to be cut regularly. And economic cycles go with ups and downs. Which implies that every once in a while a company needs to restructure. The easier it is to do so, the quicker a company can *right size*. And the better it can prepare itself for the next up-cycle. Do you prefer to be the (co-)owner of a car company in Germany, where laid-off workers need to be paid up to two years of pay, or in the USA, where 2 weeks of pay suffices? Asking the question is answering it... Ideally, invest in regions that are business-friendly, and in companies and sectors that are ran by its executives, not by unions or politicians.

As an investor, it is also important to have **fair markets**. Markets where insider trading is a frequent occurrence are to be avoided. Fair and honest markets are an absolute requirement. Never play poker in a crooked casino, never invest in a stock market full of crooks, and never invest in corrupted countries.

Needless to say, make sure to only invest in regions that do not have a habit of nationalizing companies overnight.

Which brings us to the rule of law. For an entrepreneur, **laws need to be clear and stable**. One cannot make long-term investment commitments if the law changes all the time. A stable political environment helps. As does a fair and professional legal system, with fair judges, where disputes get timely resolved.

A sad but ironic example here is Belgium. After its elections in 2010, it took the country a world-record-breaking period of 541 days to form a government. Unexpected to a lot of observers, the Belgian economy was doing rather well during this extended period of no government. In fact, GDP growth was quite a bit higher during 2010 and 2011 than it was both before the elections and after the government was formed. Although it is hard to pinpoint one single cause for this, this can be partly attributed to the fact that during the period without a government, all laws, regulations and taxes finally remained stable for some time. Conversely, in normal times every legislation wants to push through a bunch of changes, which often create more frictions than improvements.

Another aspect to look for is information. Regions with higher **reporting requirements** are to be preferred. In the United States, quarterly earnings reports are a must-do for most listed companies. So the investor gets **timely and**

reliable information. In Europe, most companies only have to report twice a year. And the time they get for filing the information is also longer: companies are required to report within 4 months after the close of the reporting period. Which means investors sometimes have to rely on information that is more than nine months old.[30]

Which brings us to another Jens-theorem: *If Babies run around on planet earth that were not even conceived yet at the close of the previous reporting period, you don't have an investor-friendly environment.*

In the United States, companies must report within 2 or 3 months after the close of the reporting period, depending on the size of the company. And quarterly reporting is required. Which seems a lot nicer from an investor point of view.

Companies that only report information in their local language, or only do their **earnings calls in a language you don't master, provide a higher hurdle to investing**. A combination of written transcripts of earnings calls and online translating tools are a very useful tools, which lower this barrier somewhat. But for an English-speaking investor, following earnings calls for Chinese, Japanese or Swedish companies, for that matter, remain somewhat of a challenge.

And last but not least, **avoid investing in countries where the currency can fluctuate wildly overnight**. The more volatile FX is, the more difficult it is to run a company. Especially if that company needs imports or exports, of which the value is denominated in stronger currencies. All management effort that needs to be put into FX-decisions is not spent building or improving products and services.

Current world situation

For the time being, the US is scoring quite well on most aspects: Taxes are getting lowered, labor unions are not too powerful, and initiatives are underway to cut red tape. The biggest disadvantage of the region is its legal system and its suing culture. Bloomberg-columnist Matt Levine has a running gag that "everything is securities fraud": if someone buys stocks, and the company does something which causes the stock to go down, the company can and will be sued for

---

[30] close of previous reporting period + 6 months new period + up to 4 months before the reporting over the most recent period is published.

securities fraud. And any company can be sued at any time for the most ridiculous reason, with a nonzero chance of losing the case. But overall, the US is scoring rather well on most other aspects.

> **Wabash Lawsuit**
>
> In 2024, trailer producer Wabash was sued for a tragic road accident that happened in 2019, in which one of the trailers they produced was involved. A car ran into the back of a parked trailer, and both the driver and the passenger of the road car lost their lives.
>
> The trailer was built by Wabash in 2004 and was adhering to all of the safety standards of that time period. The driver of the car was intoxicated and speeding, and the two people involved were not wearing their seatbelts.
>
> Wabash lost a lawsuit though, and was ordered to pay a whopping 462 million USD in penalties, which amounts up to more than half of their market capitalization of the company.
>
> These are *"risks"* and *"uncertainties"* investors ask a somewhat higher return for, and thus needlessly increase the cost-of-capital for US businesses somewhat.

Europe on the other hand is going the wrong way from a shareholder perspective, especially concerning the red tape. Every country has its own translation of European law, every country has a bunch of specific laws, and there is a chronic trend of overregulation. And there is excessive taxation as well in a number of countries. Furthermore, language barriers also complicate life: Investors who want to follow a diversified group of European stocks need to follow earnings calls in Swedish, Finnish, Spanish, French, and—Europe's unofficial national language—bad English. But at least there is a stable currency, and a low risk of nationalization of your companies.

In that respect, China is even more difficult to invest in. Huge progress and welfare were created under Deng Xiaoping's leadership. However, current president Xi Jinping is more moving back in the direction of Mao's theories,

// QUALITY OF THE SECTOR & REGION

which and had a somewhat more questionable track record for bringing economic prosperity...

> **Educational apps in China**
>
> In July 2021, new laws restricted companies from earning money on offering K-12 educational platforms, essentially making these companies nonprofits. Which is almost like de facto nationalization. Companies like TAL Education Group lost over 90% of their value overnight.
>
> Not an ideal shareholder-friendly policy change...

As such, companies in the USA deserve higher earnings multiples compared to European or Chinese companies. But once again, that does not mean that every company in the USA is a buy, and that every Chinese company is a sell. It all depends on the price you pay, and whether or not the earnings yield covers the risk of doing business in that region.

Chapter Summary

- ▸ The qualities of a sector largely overlap the qualities one looks for in a good company: Steadily growing sectors, which are not capital intensive, have a low cyclicality, but exhibit high entry barriers. And which has wealthy clients.

- ▸ Avoid sectors that mainly thrive on government grants, that run a risk of being disrupted, or that might find themselves in the middle of a geopolitical tug-of-war.

- ▸ For regional exposure, look for business-friendly environments with low taxes, a stable and predictable rule-of-law. Fair markets are a necessity, information should be amply available, and ideally there are no language barriers.

- ▸ For emerging markets, avoid companies that are too dependent on unpredictable currency fluctuations.

CHAPTER 9

Quality of the Management

"A company's financial statements tell you where it has been. The quality of its management tells you where it's going."

- THOMAS ROWE PRICE

As mentioned in the previous chapter, if one has to choose between a quality sector or a quality management, choose for the good sector. To reference Warren Buffett once again, "*You should invest in a business that even a fool can run, because someday a fool will.*" That is not to say that the quality of the management is not important at all. On the contrary. The right management team can create enormous value, while the wrong team can destroy it in an instant. But what is good leadership, and how can you recognize it?

Investors should pay close attention to how management treats its shareholders, employees, and customers. It speaks volumes about the integrity of leadership. Look for leaders who think and act like owners, not just employees. And the management team should foster a culture of discipline, innovation, and long-term thinking. Integrity is key, as the management team should be a team that can be trusted.

Integrity and Reputation

By far the most important quality of a great leadership team is its reputation, honesty and integrity. Only buy stocks of companies lead by people you would be willing to borrow your money to. Because in the end, that's wat you are (kind of) doing: you are confining the managers with a part of your net worth, and thrust them they will make the right decisions to make your stake increase in value.

// QUALITY OF THE MANAGEMENT

Unfortunately, when a lot of money is on the line, some people tend to *forget* about their ethics and decency. Examples of questionable decisions are countless:

- In 2022, Tessenderlo, a holding company controlled by Belgian billionaire Luc Tack, launched a take-over attempt on Picanol, another company he controlled. But because his ownership stake of Picanol was over 90%, while his ownership stake in Tessenderlo only amounted to around 56%, executing the transaction at an inflated price benefited himself, at the cost of the Tessenderlo minority shareholders. As one can imagine, the final price agreed upon (by the majority shareholders of both Tessenderlo and Picanol) was not a bargain, to put it very gently.

- Peugeot Invest is a holding company 80% controlled by (the heirs of) the Peugeot family. In 2024, Peugeot Invest started paying royalties to its majority shareholders for "the right of using the Peugeot-name." Now that's an efficient way to screw over your minority shareholders: start an investment company with your own name. Go public and offer some shares to minority shareholders. Then ask royalties for the use of your name...

- There are plenty of examples of holding companies where the majority shareholder launches a takeover attempt on the entire vehicle, to buy out the minorities. Often at times when market values are depressed. All too often, parts of the holding company are resold shortly after acquiring full ownership, at much higher prices.

- Dan Snyder, majority owner of the Washington Commanders NFL team, put stickers of the team logo on his personal private jet. He charged the Commanders 4.5 million dollars for "using the advertising space on his jet." The minority investors in the team were obviously not amused...

It is important to emphasize that from a legal point of view, all these moves were allowed by laws and regulations. So as a minority investor, there is not much one can do about it. Except for trying to avoid to arrive in a situation like this in the first place. So make sure to do a very decent due diligence analysis on the ethical behavior of both the CEO and the controlling shareholders. And remember that you can't make a good deal with a bad person. So never invest in a company if you wouldn't lend money to its CEO.

(And in case of a cascade of holding companies, only invest in the one that is at the top; the one in which the majority shareholder has the largest stake. This helps ensure that you are as much as possible aligned with the interests of the controlling shareholders.)

Skin in the game

One of the most effective ways to ensure that CEOs and top management act in the best interests of shareholders is by ensuring they have **"skin in the game."** This means that executives should have a significant personal financial stake in the company. This can be the case because the CEO is a significant stock owner, because of equity-based incentives, or both.

When leadership has meaningful ownership in the business, they are more likely to make decisions that drive long-term stability and profitability, as their personal wealth is directly tied to the company's performance. The alignment between the CEO's interests and shareholders' interests reduces agency problems, where management might otherwise prioritize personal short-term benefits over shareholders' long-term interests. Additionally, investors tend to have greater confidence in companies where management is financially invested alongside them, as it signals commitment and belief in the business's future.

The best situation is when the CEO is an outright shareholder, with shares bought with his own money. Founders of the company are another good example, where the ownerships stake was built "on merit." If the value of the stock ownership far exceeds the annual paycheck, that's a plus for shareholders.

For (the many) companies where this is not the case, it is important to have a well-balanced compensation package for the CEO, that strikes the right balances: The remuneration of a CEO directly influences executive decision-making, and thus shareholder value creation. A well-structured compensation package aligns the interests of executives with those of shareholders, ensuring that leadership prioritizes long-term company success over short-term financial gains.

// QUALITY OF THE MANAGEMENT

Targets looking at share price, EBIT growth or a combination of revenue growth and profitability margins are excellent. Companies where the CEO pay is based mainly on revenue or growth targets without taking into account profitability measures are to be avoided. In fact, these managers get incentivized to launch large takeover offers, *whatever the price...*

An eye should also be kept on the size of the remuneration. Especially for companies without a reference shareholder, but also in case of a founder/CEO as majority shareholder, verify that the compensation package is not excessive. Too many companies dilute their shareholders by generously handing out extremely large option packages to their executive committee.

Communication

Details

The second important thing to check regarding the management of a company one wants to invest in is corporate communication.

Some companies have managers that know every single detail about the business. On earnings calls, they can easily throw out details about production processes, filling rates of their trucks, the impact of air conditioning in factories on employee retention rates, et cetera. Other CEOs can talk for ten minutes straight, using nothing but hollow words that do not make the investors any wiser. To put it bluntly, invest in companies lead by nerds, and avoid the ones led by corporate bullshitters...

The only notable exception is in businesses that do lots of business with governments. If you are an IT-consulting company like Sopra Steria, or a defense contractor like Indra Sistema, being able to keep talking, and using large but empty words, might actually win you contracts. But these are about the only examples we can think of...

Timely communication, especially when there's bad news

Another important aspect is a timely communication. Nobody likes to bring bad news. But that is not an excuse for postponing communication, or to avoid communicating the bad news altogether.

Bad things happen. That is unavoidable when doing business, and not necessarily the management's fault. When giving an outlook over the next year, or even over the next quarter, there is inherently an aspect of uncertainty, and things don't always work out as planned. But when that happens, it should be communicated timely and openly. Avoid companies with huge negative earnings surprises without giving any warning. And if they give a warning, it should be communicated as soon as possible.

Ekopak

Belgian water recycling company Ekopak announced on 10 December 2024 that its revenue for the year, originally estimated between EUR 70-75 million, was now expect to be in the range of EUR 55-57 million.

That can happen. We are not giving critique on the original forecast or on the business results itself[31], although it ended up being way too optimistic. But clearly, the company knew, or should have known, that it would miss its annual revenue target way earlier than 3 weeks before the end of the year. But the management opted to wait with the communication, for reasons one doesn't really understand. Investments in companies with a communication like this are to be avoided.

That being said, on January 25th the company announced that it had parted ways with its CFO, which is a plus for the board of directors: it recognized the unacceptable behavior and acted accordingly.

Track record

Do not forget to investigate the track record of the management team of a company you potentially want to invest in. Questions to ask yourself with relation to the CEO, CFO, and COO are the following:

---

[31] Although it did end up being way too optimistic. If this is a one-off, it can happen. Sometimes business ends up being slower than anticipated, or contract biddings of which management thought it would win, are ultimately lost. But if this is a pattern, and management always overpromises and underdelivers, it goes without saying that this counts as a red flag too...

// QUALITY OF THE MANAGEMENT

- Has the management team already been in place for a long period of time? If the company you are looking at has a good track record, that's a positive. But was this track record obtained by the current management team, or did a previous CEO build that track record? If the person who built that track record recently left the company and moved on to a competitor, that's clearly a minus...
- Are the managers loyal to the company they work for? Or are some of them job hoppers who change jobs every two or three years?
- If the managers were recently working at another company, how did that company perform during their tenure? Because in the end, good management reflects in good numbers...
- And if the managers were recently working at another company, what was the reason for leaving?
    - The worst reason is that they were fired because of bad performance.
    - And arguably the best reason one can find is that they left their previous company because it was acquired by a larger competitor. It is a sign that the managers put the interests of the shareholders before their own interests, instead of clinging on to the CEO job and fighting against any takeover attempts.

Another aspect to keep an eye on is the general personality of the leadership team. Some people are always optimistic. Which leads to too many disappointing earnings reports, compensated by an optimistic outlook. Although a bit of ambition in the management team generally doesn't hurt, managers who always overpromise and underdeliver are to be avoided. Also, companies that report "adjusted earnings", and become more creative in finding additional adjustments every quarter are to be avoided. It can also be a sign that the managers are more focused on their (short term) share price, than on how the company is actually performing under the hood.

Other teams always seem too pessimistic or prefer to give a very prudent guidance. Often, these teams outperform their overly optimistic counterparts on the long run...

The impact of the CEO

The impact of the CEO on the performance of a company is not to be underestimated. To illustrate this with just one example, take a look at the stock price of Adidas, before and after CEO Bjørn Gulden took over the reins of the company in January 2023.

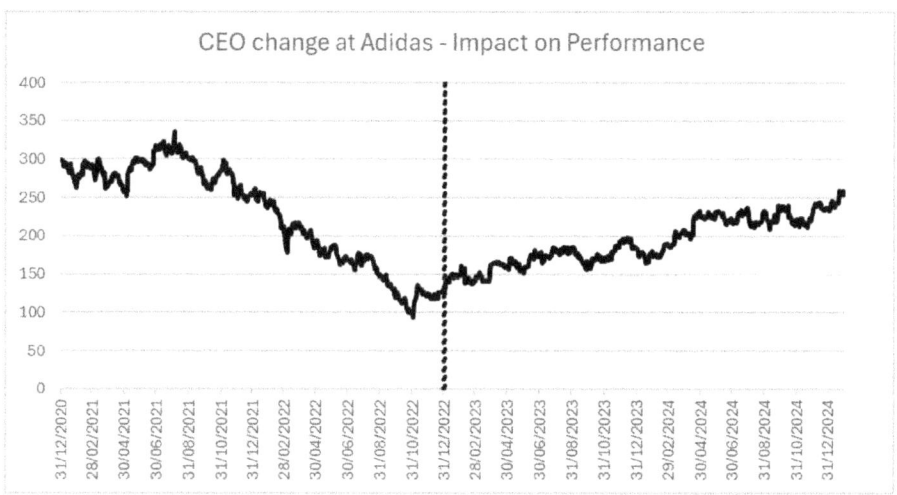

Soon after taking the reins, the operational performance of the company improved quarter after quarter, and in 2024 the earnings forecasts were raised three times during the year. Adidas shares gained 85% over the two-year period following his appointment. Equally remarkable, the shares of Puma—the company he left—dropped 22% over that same time period.

A CEO who works hard and underpromises but overdelivers is worth its weight in gold.

In another example, Starbucks stock shot up by more than 25% on August 13th 2024, because Brian Niccol was appointed CEO and chairman of the board. After doing an excellent job at Chipotle, expectations were high. At the time of writing the jury is still out on whether he will be able to turn things around, and thus whether or not the stock's reaction is justified. But the point should be clear: the leadership of the company can have a huge influence on the prospects and value of companies...

// QUALITY OF THE MANAGEMENT

The first earnings report of a new CEO is often disappointing

In the previous examples, the stock price appreciated almost immediately after the appointment of the new CEO. In the case of Starbucks, the guy hadn't even started yet. Even the announcement was sufficient to make the stock price change directions.

That being said, often—also when non-star CEOs get assigned as successor of a CEO that got fired—the first earnings report after a new CEO takes the helm disappoints somewhat. Because the new leader often wants to make his or her mark, or at least make a fresh start, restructurings are being announced, and goodwill is written off. And because this performance can be defended towards the board as "caused by previous management," the new CEO has all incentives to write down as much as possible, take out all proverbial trash cans, and start with a very conservative performance outlook.

Often, this is when the turnaround really starts, and it can be an interesting moment to pick up a hidden gem.

Chapter Summary

The leadership of a company has a large influence on the performance of a company and its stocks. Of utmost importance is the integrity and honesty of the management. Other aspects to keep an eye on are:

- Does the management have skin in the game? Preferably the CEO is also a large shareholder.
- How are managers rewarded? What is the CEO's compensation package based on?
- How does the company communicate? And is bad news brought swiftly?
- Are there job hoppers in the company's management team, or is the focus truly on the long term?
- What does the management's track record look like?

CHAPTER 10
The Other Shareholders

> *"A minority shareholder is like a passenger on a ship – choose your captain wisely."*
>
> – CHARLIE MUNGER

Throughout this book, stocks are analyzed based on a "full company" basis. As an investor, the value of the entire company is estimated. The share price is then calculated by subtracting the debt from the enterprise value, and by dividing the outcome by the number of shares in circulation. In reality, however, most individuals are only buying a small part of the company. And although (most often) the shares give the holder voting rights, in reality, one holds insufficient such rights to really weigh in on the decisions brought on the annual shareholders meeting. Thus, it is somewhat important to know who the other shareholders are, how their incentives are aligned (or misaligned) with yours, and what the consequences of this are, or can be. In what follows, a number of different situations are listed, together with the main consequences.

Types of "other shareholders"

No significant shareholders

Many listed companies have no majority shareholder[32]. In these cases, the largest ETF providers (Blackrock, Vanguard, State Street) are often the ones holding the largest positions in the company.

The advantage of having no large shareholder is that at any time a competitor or private equity company can launch a takeover attempt—which needs to be made

---

[32] In this chapter, 'majority shareholder' refers broadly to any large shareholder with enough voting power to influence a company's direction. This doesn't always require a >50% stake, as many shareholders don't vote in general meetings, allowing de-facto control with as little as 20-50% ownership.

// THE OTHER SHAREHOLDERS

at a premium to the last stock price—and there is no major shareholder there to block this from happening. Assuming the management did not introduce so-called "poison pills," mechanisms to make an acquisition more difficult, in the bylaws of the company.

This immediately leads us to the most negative point: it can be very difficult to replace bad management or make changes to the board of directors. There is nobody weighing in on the decision-making, making it easier for managers to enrich themselves by granting themselves large renumerations and option packages. In particular, if the CEO is also the chairman, or if the chairman is not independent, this is a danger at companies without a significant shareholder. The only thing that can introduce change is either an activist building up a large stake before pushing for changes, or a competitor or private equity firm launching a takeover attempt.

For smaller companies, liquidity is also worth noting. Having a 100% free float will give the stock better liquidity, compared to a situation where large quantities of the stock are owned by one controlling shareholder.

An activist bought a significant stake

If a shareholder activist holds a (somewhat) large stake, this can be a good thing. Most activist investors are pushing for improvements at the company level and try to maximize shareholder value. If the management is open to cooperating with the activist investor, this is often a win for all parties involved (including the minority shareholder).

If the conversations become less friendly, however, one can expect a period of higher uncertainty, often accompanied by more volatile stock prices. And if both the management and the activist investor are really putting their own interests first and above all else, the very worst thing that can happen is the company buying back the shares of the activist at a premium. This practice is sometimes executed with malice aforethought by corporate riders (think Carl Icahn) and is called "greenmail": the "activist" buys a stake of a couple of percentages in the company, threatens with a takeover attempt, and settles with the management to buy back the activists' shares at a premium. This reprehensible practice is illegal in a number of states and countries but is still allowed in others. Needless to say, this is the worst outcome for the minority investors: the company buys back shares at a price above the market price, bad management remains in place, leadership attention was deviated from the core business for a couple of weeks or months during this fight, and the entire episode created uncertainty for all employees in the company.

So if an activist buys a significant stake, it is usually a positive... but don't forget to verify the tone and track record of this activist investor.

Another company holding a controlling interest

This situation often occurs in carve-outs or spin-offs. A large company wants to focus on its core business and spins out divisions that are considered "non-core," either by selling shares of this newly formed separate company via an IPO, or by handing these shares out to its existing shareholders. Often, only some of the shares are sold or dispensed in the first step, with the plan to sell the remaining shares at a later date (often one to three years later).

In this situation, the investor should have some mixed feelings about the situation. The fact that the "mother company" still has shares creates a *"stock overhang"*: Everybody knows that there is a large shareholder looking to sell shares at some point in the future. As prices are formed based on demand and supply, an overhang of "supply" is negative for the stock price.

That said, spin-offs are often mispriced by the market. Either because this newly formed company gets energized by a new management/CEO and finally gets the freedom to be run in the best way possible (versus being in a dark corner of a larger conglomerate and holding the stamp of being a "non-core activity"). Or, especially relevant in the case in which the shares were handed out to the existing shareholders of the mother company, because a lot of market participants don't really want to hold these shares. Because they invested in the mother company for its core activities, and not for this side business. Or because they are an index fund or mutual fund with certain rules and regulations. They are only allowed to buy shares of companies with certain activities, or with a minimum market capitalization, criteria which the carved-out company might not fulfil. This creates "forced sellers" and depresses the stock price.

Hence, it is often a good idea to buy shares of these carve-outs, at those depressed prices, a couple of months or years after it is listed. After the forced sellers pushed the price down, or ideally around the time the mother company gets rid of its last tranche of shares it was still holding post-IPO. Because often the stock of these companies rally after the stock overhang disappears.

Private equity funds holding a controlling interest

When a private equity fund holds a large stake in the company[33], this is often positive in the short run. It means management gets a ton of pressure to perform and can count on the network of the private equity firm to increase its knowledge, create synergies, and maximize shareholder value.

If a private equity firm is already in the company's capital for a number of years[34], and did not sell shares in the open market yet, one can start hoping that the private equity firm will try to find a strategic buyer. They will try to get a take-over offer at the highest possible price, which often leads to an acquisition of the entire company, benefiting all minority shareholders equally as well. Definitely a plus.

The opposite is also true. Similar to carve-outs, a potential disadvantage is that there might be a stock overhang, especially if the private equity firm already sold tranches of shares on the open market in the previous months. It is an indication the company is looking for an exit and concluded that the best option is to sell the stock on the stock exchange. Well-run firms have a large network and will always be on the lookout to sell to either a strategic buyer, or to other private equity companies. So if stocks are sold on the open market, it is a sign that no other party was found that was willing to offer a better price than where the stock is currently trading. This certainly counts as a negative, and might lead to a stock overhang over the coming months or even years.

In those situations, one should remain very careful after the private equity firm sells its last shares in the market. Because although it makes the stock overhang disappear, it also decreases the pressure on the management to increase

---

[33] Some private equity funds do invest part of their funds in publicly listed equity.

[34] Most private equity funds have an investment horizon of around 10 years. And it often takes a couple of years between launching the fund and making their investments. Which means they will start looking to divest about 5-6 years after making their initial buy decision...

shareholder value, and the line to the strong network of the private equity firm evaporates. Furthermore, the private equity firm will have made sure that all quick wins and improvements were already implemented, leaving little room for, for example, further cost-cutting initiatives. Sometimes there might have even been a push to improve the financial figures of the company right before the PE-firm sold its stake, e.g. by pushing deliveries and invoicing right before the end of a financial quarter or year, or by postponing marketing or R&D expenses. So one should be very careful when buying stocks at a time when the sophisticated investor and insider is selling.

And lastly, if the management of the company is very good, it is not impossible for the PE-firm to try to hire the best parts of a management team away later on, when they moved on and made investments in other companies...

Long story short: private equity involvement is very good in the short run. But avoid stocks of companies in which the sophisticated investor is (or recently was) selling their shares on the open market.

The founder or CEO holding a controlling stake

Arguably, this is the best situation one can be in: investing alongside a passionate founder, who spends, and will continue to spend, all his time and energy on building out and growing the company. Often the founder already made a track record (otherwise the company wouldn't be large enough to be listed on the stock exchange) and wants to continue expanding the company.

The incentives are also aligned: the stocks in the company often make up vast majority of the wealth of the founder/CEO, so the best way to increase wealth is to create shareholder value. The monthly paycheck is often negligible compared to the total net worth of the founder.

A disadvantage is sometimes the liquidity of the stock: especially in smaller companies, if a large stake of the company is owned by the founder of the company, the free float is rather small, leading to the stock trading infrequently. Especially if you want to buy or sell a relatively large amount of stocks, your own buying/selling can move the stock price up/down. This is a situation to avoid, as it makes your average buy price higher, and sell price lower. And especially if the company announces bad news, it can be very difficult to even find someone who wants to buy your shares if you want to get out. And this might be true at any price...[35]

Depending on the age of the founder, succession plans can become a topic of interest as well. The impact of succession plans on a company largely depends on the founder's age and circumstances. If the founder has no clear successor, he may be inclined to exit the business, seeking to sell it to a private equity firm or a competitor for the highest possible price. Ideally, this sale would occur at a premium above the market value, potentially delivering a significant boost to shareholder returns.

However, challenges arise when a founder grows older and less energized yet remains unwilling to relinquish control. The situation can become even more complicated if the company becomes embroiled in a power struggle among potential successors—such as the founder's children or other family members. Internal conflicts of this nature can lead to instability, mismanagement, and, ultimately, the erosion of shareholder value.

Holding companies

A special situation occurs at holding companies. These are listed vehicles which are owning shares (or full ownership) in a number of different companies, often spread across different sectors. These are companies like Berkshire Hathaway, Boston Omaha, Prosus, Bolloré or Peugeot Invest, among others. Often, they serve as a controlling vehicle of a wealthy investor or businessman.

The advantage for a wealthy family to structure their equity stakes in a holding company can be for tax reasons (depending on the jurisdiction), to be able to hand over ownership to next generations without losing control, or to control companies with a lower amount of capital.

If you own 51% of a company that owns 51% of a company that owns 51% of an entity, you basically have full control over the board decisions of that entity, while needing less than 15% of the market value of that entity (= 0.51*0.51*0.51). Bernard Arnault, the richest man in Europe, used this technique to perfection

---

[35] The topic of liquidity will be discussed in more detail later on in this chapter.

when building his luxury empire (LVMH, owner of Louis Vuitton, Moët, Hennessy, Tiffany, and many other brands).

Another advantage of such a structure is that it trades on the markets, which means a value can be put on those shares. This can come in handy, especially when the second or third generation takes over: some family members might have a strong interest in the family conglomerate, while others may want to pursue other endeavors. Having a listed vehicle allows buying and selling but can also come in handy as a basis in determining a price if blocks of shares are traded between family members themselves. Having a listed stock price can avoid difficult and endless discussions on what the combination of businesses is actually worth.

Buying shares, and thus (often) becoming a minority shareholder in one of these vehicles or holding companies, again has advantages and disadvantages. One advantage is that it allows you to enjoy the fruitful labor of this wealthy and successful businessman. *"I might be not as smart as Warren Buffett, but I can buy shares of Berkshire Hathaway, and thus invest alongside him and generate the same investment returns as he does."* Another advantage is that often, holding companies are traded at a discount compared to the sum of the underlying assets. This means you can "buy on the cheap."

The main disadvantage, and the main reason for the discount, is that you have no control over the company. And worse: someone else does! As long as the incentives of the controlling shareholder are aligned with yours, which means maximizing the return of the holding company, there is no issue. Same thing if the controlling shareholder is a gentleman of character. (Think Warren Buffett.)

Unfortunately, when a lot of money is on the line, most people tend to *forget* about their ethics and decency. Examples of questionable decisions are countless. We refer to the examples given in the first section of chapter 9…

Our advice: when investing in family-controlled holding companies, make sure to do a very decent due diligence analysis on the ethical behavior of the controlling shareholder. And in case of a cascade of holding companies, only invest in the one that is on top; the one in which the family has the largest stake. To ensure that you are as much as possible aligned with the interests of the controlling shareholders.

Also, try to assess the financial situation of this controlling shareholder: if he/she took large personal loans to finance investments and comes under financial pressure, one can be sure the decisions taken in the holding company will reflect the personal financial needs of this one shareholder, rather than be in the best interest of the holding company itself.

Furthermore, keep an eye on the cost structure of the holding company itself: investment vehicles in which too much value flows towards its management team – often members of the controlling shareholder – are to be avoided.

Share Classes and Voting Rights

In an ideal world, or in the ideal company, there is only one share class. Which implies that one share has one voting right. This aligns the voting rights with the economic incentives. The more shares you have, the more voting power. And if you want to control the company, you need to have more than half of the shares outstanding. Not all shareholders will vote. So a de facto majority can be reached with a slightly lower percentage as well. But you get the point.

The last couple of decades, however, it became more and more popular to create different share classes, with each share class holding different voting rights. This allows the founders of the company to sell a large number of stocks and cash in, but still keep control over the company by holding special shares which were assigned super voting power.

For example, Facebook has A and B shares. The economic rights of both share classes are identical. The only difference is that the A shares have one voting right per share, while the B-class has 10 voting rights per share. Most of the B shares are held by Mark Zuckerberg. At the time of writing, Mark holds *only* about 14% of the shares of Facebook. But because of different share classes, he still holds approximately 60% of the voting power and thus has full control over the company.

Although this doesn't automatically mean that the company is bad, or that the management is full of crooks, it does leave at least a bit of a bad taste: some shareholders appear to be *worth* more than others. And it can be very difficult to change the leadership or the board, in these kinds of setups. Which means that there is a higher risk that the company is not managed to optimize shareholder value. And that, in companies where this is no longer the case, it can be very hard to mend the situation.

> **The example of Oil-Dri:**
>
> A notable situation occurs at Oil-Dri Corporation of America. This company, a producer of cat litter and other moisture absorption products, does have A and B shares. And the B shares have 10x more voting power than the A shares. This is similar to the set-up at Meta. However, the A shares receive 133.33% of the dividends of the B-shares. This looks like a fair deal: the family wants to retain in control of the company but agrees to "pay" a little something for this privilege. One can debate what the voting power is worth. Usually, it is worth nothing until the moment it becomes worth a lot, e.g. in case of a merger attempt, or if a shareholder activist shows up at the front door. But the least you can say is that this setup, in which the controlling shareholder agrees to pay up for control, is an indication that the management is handling in good faith with relation to its other shareholders.

Market Liquidity and Volatility

Active investing and stock picking is less and less popular these days. As a result, interest in small cap stocks is waning. This decreases the liquidity (the amount of money traded) in these stocks, which leads to advantages and disadvantages.

The biggest disadvantage is that it becomes more difficult to invest large amounts of money in these stocks: If only 20k USD is traded per day, it is difficult to build up a position of 100k USD in that stock: the price of the stock will go up considerably, just because you are buying, which is to be avoided. Furthermore, if something bad happens to the company and you want to sell, probably a lot of other people will come to the same conclusion as you and will rush to sell. Lots of sellers, and no buyers, means no transactions can be executed, except if substantially lower prices would draw some buyers' interest. (But if nobody is following that stock, then even lower prices might not lure too many investors...) Investing in listed equity without the ability to exit is to be avoided.

// THE OTHER SHAREHOLDERS

The very same thing leads to two advantages. One: a lot of professional investors (mutual funds, insurance companies, ...) won't even bother to follow these companies. Because they cannot invest the amounts of money they need to invest without moving the price considerably. Which means you are competing against less sophisticated shareholders trading in the stock. And which often means the company is trading at lower multiples than large companies. So you can buy the same earnings power *on the cheap*.

And two: price movements in illiquid stocks tend to be larger. Some people will see this as a disadvantage. They interpret large volatility with large risk and run scared. But if you are an investor with a somewhat longer time horizon, you can exploit those larger price movements to your advantage. Be patient, and you might be able to buy the stocks at an incredibly low price you thought would be impossible. And the opposite is also true: if someone starts buying larger amounts of stocks without paying too much attention, he or she might move up the price considerably. This allows you to cash in by selling some of your shares to the chap who really wanted those shares badly and immediately... (In the end, everyone gets what they want, right? You're doing the investors' equivalent of charitable work!) Just make sure you can stomach large price fluctuations, even at times when there is absolutely no news concerning the company you are invested in.

In summary, investing in less liquid stocks has both advantages and disadvantages. For individuals or smaller investors, there is a sweet spot here: invest in companies that have a sufficient level of liquidity for your investment size. But which are too small for institutional investors. As such, you can still freely move in or out, while large institutional investors don't have that option. But **avoid investing in companies with too low of liquidity!** If your view on the company turns south, you absolutely want to make sure you have a way out...

> ### Worst of both worlds
>
> Investing in private equity gives the advantage of control: the PE-investor typically cooperates with management, or even has a seat in the board of directors, to try to steer the company in the right direction. If the performance of the company turns sour, one can try to turn things around.

In listed equity, investors most often don't have that ability: you are too small of a shareholder to have a meaningful influence or voting power, and although some hedge funds do manage to score board seats, most investors in listed equity cannot weigh in in how a company is run. So if things turn sour, the listed equity investor cannot try to solve the problem. But he can sell his shares. Which is something that cannot be easily done by his private equity counterpart.

An investor in illiquid listed equity combines the worst of both worlds: no real voting power, because you are a minority shareholder in a listed company. And you have no ability to quickly sell your shares, because there is no volume; there are no buyers. Needless to say, situations like this should be avoided. Because if the company starts performing badly, you literally have no good options to choose from. The only way to avoid a situation like this? Avoid investing in illiquid stocks.

Note however that the previous section discusses *average* volatility throughout the year. Because liquidity varies over the course of the year. E.g. during the Christmas period and during summer breaks, fewer portfolio managers and traders are at their desks managing their portfolios and trading stock. This *temporarily* reduces the liquidity on the markets. This is nothing to be afraid of, and savvy investors can use this to their advantage: lower liquidity levels often cause elevated levels of price volatility. One or two larger orders can move market prices up or down during those periods. So if someone really wants to buy or sell a relatively large number of shares, the price of shares might arrive at levels you thought were impossible. So it can be interesting to be in the market at those times, using limit orders at optimistic prices (low when buying, high when selling), and hope they get executed.

Reasons for those large buyers or sellers might be:

- for tax-loss harvesting reasons
- forced sellers, people who need the money
- index reshufflings (although index providers tend to avoid reshuffling the index weights during holiday periods)

▸ during holiday periods, uninformed retail investors form a relatively larger part of the trading volume than during normal working periods. Bored retail investors browsing the internet might read some rumors or memes and buy stocks or options without any fundamental analysis or estimation of the value of the underlying company.

It is important to keep a crucial distinction in mind: be on the lookout to buy shares of small and midcaps during periods of the year of lower liquidity (e.g. Christmas), but never buy stocks that are too illiquid—for the position you want to build up in the stock—throughout the year. And always use limit orders when trading less-liquid stocks, to avoid negative surprises of causing market moves yourself!

It is important to keep this key distinction in mind: strategically seek opportunities to purchase shares of small- and mid-cap companies during periods of lower market liquidity, such as the holiday season around Christmas. These times can often present attractive entry points due to temporarily reduced trading activity. However, while taking advantage of these moments, one must be cautious never to invest in stocks that are excessively illiquid throughout the year, relative to the size of the position you intend to build. Attempting to do so can lead to significant execution challenges and potential difficulties when trying to exit the investment later on.

Additionally, always ensure that you use limit orders when trading less liquid stocks. This precaution helps protect against unexpected price fluctuations and prevents you from inadvertently moving the market against yourself.

Chapter Summary

When investing in listed equity, you are not the only shareholder. Therefore, you can be affected by actions and decisions taken by your fellow shareholders. A number of situations were listed.

▸ If there is no majority shareholder, takeover attempts by competitors or private equity firms are always a possibility. The disadvantage is that nobody is really controlling the management and the board of directors.

- Activist investors as majority shareholders are often good: the activist will put pressure on the management to create shareholder value. A disadvantage is that greenmail is a possible outcome if the relationship between management and the activist investor is toxic.

- If a holding is a majority owner, the situation is similar as with activist investors. Except that the probability of toxic relations of lower. Most holding companies only invest on friendly terms, while some activist investors opt for a more offensive approach.

- If another company is the largest shareholder (e.g. after a spin-off or carve-out) this is a negative sign, because there is a stock overhang.

- The same thing is true with private equity. But as long as they remain a shareholder, it should be a plus, as the focus will be on creating shareholder value. Consider selling if the PE-fund is selling, though. It could be an indication that the company is performing optimally, which implies the upside potential is gone…

- Founders as majority shareholders are a big plus, as long as the remuneration for the founder/CEO is not extravagant.

Only invest in holding companies if the minority shareholders get treated fairly. Corporate governance is especially important if the majority shareholder is a family controlling the vehicle. If you get treated fairly, investing alongside families can deliver truly wonderful returns. But the risk of getting taken for a ride as a minority shareholder is not negligible.

Also keep an eye on liquidity. Never invest in listed equity if there is no way out. But there might be a sweet spot of smaller companies with sufficient liquidity for your needs, which are too illiquid for large institutional investors.

Keep an eye on the stock markets during holiday periods (if your family allows). Larger price fluctuations are possible, without any company news or change in fundamentals, which can lead to unexpected opportunities.

CHAPTER 11

When Should You Sell a Stock?

> *"It's not whether you're right or wrong that's important, but how much money you make when you're right and how much you lose when you're wrong."*
>
> - GEORGE SOROS

A lot of ink has been spent on when to buy a stock. However, an equally difficult, or arguably even harder decision to make is when to sell a stock. Contrary to picking up fresh new stocks, the ones that are already in your portfolio can cause a number of biases: you thought it was a buy in the past, so selling can feel like admitting that you were wrong. Especially if the current stock price is below the point where it was bought. Biases like this can cost investors a lot of money in the long run, so a number of these pitfalls will be discussed throughout this chapter. But first, a number of valid reasons to sell a stock are listed.

Good reasons to sell a stock

Cut your losses

The rationally easiest decision might be mentally the hardest one: it's the famous "cut your losses" case. You bought a stock, and the performance of the company went down or wasn't what you expected. Sell!!! The costliest mistake is to keep your losers in your portfolio. The faster you take the decision, the better.

As Peter Lynch put it: *"Some people automatically sell the winners and hold on to their losers ... which is about as sensible as pulling out the flowers and watering the weeds."*

// WHEN SHOULD YOU SELL A STOCK?

Notice that I wrote "performance of the company." I did not list "stock performance." Sometimes a stock just gets hammered down without apparent reason. As long as the underlying company performance and prospects remain good, don't worry too much about short-term fluctuations in the stock price.

Avoid using stop-loss orders[36]. In today's markets, an increasing share of trading is driven by algorithms that rely on stop-loss mechanisms and momentum-based strategies. These automated trades often feed off each other, amplifying market movements in response to relatively minor news. As a result, what might otherwise be a small dip can quickly snowball into an exaggerated price swing. Rather than selling into such volatility, these moments can sometimes present attractive buying opportunities, provided that the company's underlying performance remains solid. Before acting, always assess whether the fundamentals justify taking advantage of the market overreaction.

While one argues throughout this book that markets are not efficient, it does not mean markets are stupid. More often than not, falling stock prices are at least a sign that market conditions are changing, or that the future looks less bright than it did before. So while a falling stock price should not lead to an automatic sell decision, its signal should not be neglected either: Use this sign as an opportunity to do your homework over one more time. Think and rethink: are you missing something? Is the market seeing something that you are not? If, after breaking your head for a day or two, the answer is no, then go for it and buy the dip.

Also cut if you don't have losses

If a company is underperforming your original expectations, don't keep the stock in your portfolio because the stock price is not down yet. The argument might sound silly, but there are plenty of examples of stocks that publish bad earnings, after which the stock price remains flat or even increases for a couple of days, and only later on starts to gradually see its value erode. This is often not in a dramatic fashion: no 20% drop in one day. But 1 or 2% per day for a couple of weeks has the same effect on your portfolio returns, without catching newspapers' atten-

---

[36] Stop-loss orders are orders to automatically sell a stock once its price drops below a certain value. It avoids further losses, but when stock markets are very volatile, you often end up selling stocks at the worst possible moment: when the price hits its bottom.

tion. Long story short: if the performance of the company is not in line with your initial expectations, and therefore breaking your initial investment case, the decision should be obvious: sell.

Let your profits run

The opposite case is the most enjoyable one. But it's also a hard nut to crack: you bought a great company at a good or even cheap price. The stock went up in a dramatic fashion. Now it becomes fairly valued, or even reaches a high valuation. This leads to the question: when to sell?

If you sell too soon, people will tell you that *"you should let your profits run."* But if you don't sell, and the price comes back to earth, you'll hear that *"you shouldn't extrapolate"* & *"You can't expect the trees to grow to the sky."* Acing the perfect moment is almost impossible: very rarely does an investor manage to exactly sell at the top. Which means every decision to sell almost automatically leads to a regret in the next few days or weeks: "if I only held on to it for a little while longer..."

A wise investor and friend of the author uses the following trick to overcome this tendency: He genuinely wants the person who buys your stock to also have the opportunity to make a small profit. So if you are someone who has difficulties selling stocks that went up considerably and are now rationally overvalued, this mental trick is worth trying. Maybe it can help you.

Far more often though, investors don't sell their winners too late, but (way) too soon. Which can be a very costly mistake. You can never expect to have a four-bagger if you sell all your stocks as soon as they go up by 20%... The easiest way to cope with this tendency is to make an estimation of the intrinsic value of the stock at the time of buying, and to keep adjusting your estimation as new information becomes available. So at every quarterly update, if the performance of the company (not the stock!) was better than expected, or if the outlook is raised above your initial expectations, your estimation of the intrinsic value is to be adjusted upwards accordingly. (It also works the other way around!)

If you bought the stock at a 50% discount of your estimated intrinsic value, the stock should double in value before you start feeling temptation to sell. Which means you shouldn't even be thinking about selling after a 20% gain. On the contrary, you should be tempted to buy more, especially if the company reports earnings in line with, or better than, your original investment case. Let your profits run. As long as the company does what you expected it to do, that is...

Also looking at how the stock is valued compared to its own historical multiples can help to convince yourself to keep holding your best horses. Making peer comparisons can also help.

All of this can be summarized as follows: a company and its management should:

- Show you the money: a company should be profitable, and it should be obvious where the cash is generated.
- Keep you happy: the original investment case should remain in place to hold on to a stock.
- And don't lie to you: if management lies and either overpromises or does not deliver on earlier goals, it is time to reconsider your position.

If all three are still fulfilled, and the stock is not exceeding your estimate of intrinsic value: just relax and enjoy the ride! But... always be on the lookout for red flags too. Which is the topic of the next section.

Red Flags

In this section, a number of red flags are discussed. It concerns topics to be aware of and to pay attention to. And while one or two red flags might not alter the investment decision, it may be interesting to postpone your investment decision until some of these flags disappear. If a whole bunch of red flags are raised, the better option might be to sell, and search for another company to invest in instead...

Negative Earnings Revisions

The first red flag is the easiest to understand: negative earnings revisions are a bad sign. It means business is less good than the management originally anticipated. Worse, if you took chapter 9 seriously, it means the companies you are invested in have a conservative management that has a habit of underpromising and overdelivering. So if management is known as such, negative revisions[37] should definitely raise a flag.

Remarkably, when the business of a company starts to slow down, an earnings revision seldomly comes alone. Most often bad news is delivered in three slices. The first earnings revision is often a small one. The business starts slowing down, but the management is often very optimistic by nature (otherwise you don't end up as a businessman) and thinks this is a temporary slowdown and the market will recover. Sometimes this is preceded by an earnings report in which earnings were below target, but the target for the year is reaffirmed "because things will be better in three to six months from now." The second negative earnings revision is a more serious one, in which it begins to dawn on management that they were too optimistic. The negative momentum cannot be denied anymore, and the CEO is forced to lower the targets. But all too often management is either still too optimistic, or too afraid to go to the board and present them the realities of the day. They need a couple of months more, during which no recovery occurs (on the contrary, markets are contracting) to let reality fully sink in and leads to a third earnings warning. This one often goes paired with an overreaction in the other direction: Normally upbeat and positive CEOs now become more and more depressed and alter the earnings outlook dramatically. This is often the point during which all the bad news (and more?) gets factored in, and it might be a good point for contrarian investors to start buying the stock.

Long story short: a first negative earnings revision—even a modest one—is to be interpreted as a red flag. Because all too often it's an underestimation of the real troubles boiling below.

---

[37] Below managements' expectations, that is. (Results below market consensus estimates are not necessarily a red flag, if those estimates were out-of-line with managements' visions.)

// WHEN SHOULD YOU SELL A STOCK?

Don't be in a hurry to buy after multiple negative outlook adjustments

Many investment decisions at institutional investors are made at committees. These are scheduled on fixed days of the week and need some sort of consensus before actions get taken. Thus, these investors are naturally slow in the decision-making process.

So contrary to efficient market theories, not all (good or bad) news gets immediately factored in. Reactions (and overreactions) are slow in nature, which is just one of the reasons why stocks are momentum-driven. What goes up keeps going up. And what goes down often keeps going down. Even after all the good or bad news is already published[38].

So even if a stock appears to be overreacting to a negative earnings report and you are willing to buy at today's prices, often there is time to pick up the stock. And the negative momentum surrounding the stock might lead to even better prices in the days following the bad earnings report. Don't rush, and consider buying gradually over the days and weeks after the bad news is published.

Accounting scams

Saying that one shouldn't invest in accounting scams is like kicking in an open door. The difficulty lies in the fact that most[39] companies obviously don't say they are running an accounting scam. So here is a list containing a number of indicators to help assess whether or not a company might be running an accounting scam. And remember: If the numbers look too good to be true, they generally are...

> ▸ Calculate the revenue and the profit a company is generating per employee. And judge whether or not this looks plausible.

---

[38] Usually brokers also revise their target values and recommendations a couple of days after the company published its earnings report. Which leads to a continuation of the (good or bad) news flows surrounding the company for a couple of days more...

[39] Surprisingly, not all of them! E.g. (now fallen) crypto king Sam Bankman-Fried explained, to a stunning detail, how his company FTX was actually running a Ponzi scheme during Bloomberg podcast "Odd Lots." The guy is sentenced to 25 years in prison now...

- Make that same calculation with regards to PP&E. If the number is lower than the amount needed to give all employees a laptop, in a sector where everyone works at an office, I've got news for you...
- If the company frequently changes its revenue recognition standards, it might be better to stay on the sidelines.
- If depreciation and amortization are suspiciously low, the company might be hiding the true costs, to bump up accounting earnings.
- Capitalizing expenses: Companies can inflate earnings by classifying expenses as assets, spreading costs over many years instead of recognizing them immediately. If lots of expenses get capitalized, watch out...
- If accounting receivables consistently grow faster than revenues, fake sales or aggressive revenue recognition may be in play.
- An auditor delay or a report with "concerns" or "limitations" is a very serious red flag.
- If management dodges analyst or investor questions, refuses interviews, or limits earnings call Q&A, they may have something to hide.

Beware of (soft) accounting manipulations

Besides these hard accounting scams, there are also a number of *soft* manipulations a management can do. These management decisions make a company look better than it actually is, for a short period of time. These are not illegal activities, but they might deceive the analyst nonetheless. Let's call them "accounting cosmetics."

Marketing and R&D expenses are the easiest ones the management of a company can use to manipulate short-term earnings. If the projected earnings will not be reached (and thereby, potentially, endangering the bonus of the management), a "quick fix" can be to cut in the advertising budget, or scale down the R&D budget. These measures lead to an immediate reduction in the costs—and hence bump up profit margins—while their effect on revenue growth of the company often only kicks in with a certain delay. R&D projects are *only* impacting earnings in the next product cycle, which might only be launched a couple of quarters or even years down the road. And although innovation might be necessary for a company to survive, it could be very tempting for a certain type of manager to give up some longer-term prospects of the company in order to make a quick gain. Especially if the manager is close to retirement, looking for another job, or has a large stock option plan expiring...

It is important to note that not all managers are *crooks*. Most CEOs live and breathe the company and do their utmost best to create a good track record on the long run. Sometimes, especially if the company goes through difficult times, scaling back on all sorts of expenses might be necessary, and an indication of GOOD management. E.g. airlines stopping marketing initiatives shortly after Covid kicked in made total sense. On the contrary, not cutting back on advertising dollars when the government forbids flying would have been an indication of bad management. But in the absence of a cash crunch for the company, a dramatic and unannounced reduction of R&D and marketing spending which magically leads to earnings just falling within the guided range should raise a red flag.

In general, a founder and family owner CEO of the company will be less inclined to do such trickery, even if he or she is close to retirement. A founder often has pride in what was built and keeps thinking long term (e.g. wealth for future generations).

On the other end of the spectrum, we find private equity firms who invested in the company eight or nine years ago[40] and are looking for an exit. These funds have an incentive to try to bump up the stock price (and certainly to avoid a stock crash) just at the moment they want to exit the position. So if a company is mainly owned and managed by a private equity firm looking to exit, be very careful.

Once again, it is important to keep in mind that not everyone is unscrupulous. But it's never bad to keep some healthy suspicions in those circumstances. As Uncle Charlie often said: *"Show me the incentives and I'll show you the outcome. It's that simple."*

ERP Upgrades

Large companies that update their ERP systems are a red flag. You cannot imagine the number of companies that managed to screw up such upgrades. For

---

[40] Most private equity funds have a targeted investment horizon of 10 to 12 years.

one reason or another, such systems only seem to work if they grow organically. Organically grown software code might look ugly from the outside, but if it works, the best advice is often to keep your hands off. If it ain't broke, don't fix it...

Don't get me wrong. There might be situations in which it can be a good idea for a large company to upgrade their ERP systems. Especially if the company's systems are very old. Or if the company made a number of acquisitions over the years, and never really managed to merge or to integrate the different software systems into one package. Or if the introduction of additional technology can lead to more efficient production lines and inventory management. (E.g. cameras, IoT and AI integration can optimize production lines, et cetera). But you cannot imagine the number of companies that managed to screw up an ERP system upgrade. All too often, these programs run over budget and over time. If not worse.

For example, Lamb Weston, market leader in frozen potato products (think French fries), managed to screw up the upgrade of their central system. For over a week, the American operations of the company were severely disturbed. The company had no clue which customer orders were fulfilled, which factory produced what, and how much inventory was stored where. A large number of clients did not receive their orders, causing restaurants to run out of supply of French fries. Obviously, this led to penalty payments for breaches of contracts, unhappy customers, and a permanent loss of market share. It even attracted an activist hedge fund (Jana Partners), which tried to overthrow the entire board of the company.

If a company announces big plans to upgrade the entire ERP-system, there is only one advice: RUN!

Unfaithful Management

One of the things your author is allergic to is managers complaining about their share price being too low, instead of spending their energy in actions that create shareholder value. But that only counts as an orange flag.

Every once in a while though, some people take it one step further. Just one example: Jeffrey Lorberbaum, CEO of Mohawk Industries, on the Q2 2023 earnings call on July 26th: "*We're confident that the markets are going to recover.*

// WHEN SHOULD YOU SELL A STOCK?

We can't predict the moment, but we know they're going to recover. So it's a good time to buy shares." The company is also buying back its own shares on the market.

A couple of days later, on July 29 and July 30, CEO Lorberbaum sold a combined 14,200 shares for 2.3 million USD. And although Mr. Lorberbaum remains a large shareholder of the company, the least one can say is that it gives us a bit of a bad taste, and gives the impression that the remarks on the call were a way to try to pump up the share price a bit, right before selling stocks himself. Of course there can be valid reasons why the CEO needed to sell some shares or needed cash money. But it's not a good look, to say the least.

The Mohawk example is just one illustration; more importantly, this is not an isolated case. **If you see very positive comments from the management of a company, and at the same time insider selling, this should be a red flag for investors**. The same goes for aggressive share buybacks executed by the company, with company managers selling shares during the same timeframe.

Rapid changes in the leadership of a company

If there are a lot of changes in C-level positions or on the board of a company, that is a red flag, at least for companies that appear to be performing well from an outside view. Maybe the insiders know something that the general public doesn't know yet? Maybe there is a toxic leadership situation at the top, and corporate politics are played dirty? Anyway, if lots of people are suddenly leaving a well-performing company, it is a red flag.

(Obviously, a lot of changes in a bad-performing company, or a badly-led company, are a plus. But in this chapter, we are discussing sell decisions. And you shouldn't own companies that have bad management in place... 😊)

Insider Sales

If insiders are selling shares, this can be a red flag. But one should not take this one too strongly. As long as management has skin in the game, that's OK.

There can be thousands of reasons for insiders to sell shares, without having anything to do with negative views on the company. Maybe that person needs to pay down a house, car, boat, or a kid's tuition. Maybe the person is tax harvesting.

Maybe the person has an overallocation of his net worth in his employers' stock—which naturally happens if a large part of the compensation is paid in stock options—and wants to diversify his or her equity holdings. None of these need to imply something negative for our company.

However, if many investors sell large parts of their stock holdings, that is undoubtedly a negative sign. And—as discussed earlier—if this happens at a time when the company is massively buying back its own shares, it smells like a pump-and-dump, and is definitely a red flag.

> **Insider buying**
>
> While there might be a thousand reasons for insiders to sell stocks, there is only one reason why insiders buy stocks: because they think the stock will appreciate in value. So **insider buying is a dark green flag**, and a very positive sign.
>
> That being said, it only counts if it concerns a significant amount. A well-paid manager who buys 2,000 USD worth of shares is not to be interpreted as a positive, but rather as an attempt to be mentioned in the list of insider buyers. This is more of a sign that the manager is focused on manipulating the stock price upwards, rather than on managing the company to create long-term value.

Behavioral biases

While it is rather easy to write down a list of reasons to sell a stock, the key is in the execution, in actually following and applying these rules. It might all sound straightforward, but human beings—even analysts and professional investors—are far from 100% rational in their decision-making process. A company in which you have already invested and have been following for an extended period can subtly pull you into various behavioral biases. Your familiarity with the stock might lead to overconfidence in your assessment, causing you to overlook warning signs or rationalize poor performance. Emotional attachment can also make it harder to reassess your position objectively, increasing the risk of holding onto a struggling investment longer than you should. Recognizing these biases is crucial to making rational, fact-based decisions rather than being swayed by past commitments or personal attachment.

One of these biases is the **myopic bias**: falling in love with the stock. People value something they already have at a higher value than what they don't have. This is obviously not rational, but it is an easy trap to fall into. Also, you liked the stock before—otherwise you would not have bought it—so selling feels a bit like "changing your mind." Even if the stock price went up, or if the fundamentals of the company deteriorated, and thus even if the investment case changed completely. You also know the company better and listened to the company's management and their story every quarter. This makes it easier to just hold on to the stock for one more quarter, because the story often sounds compelling. Don't fall for it. It is important to keep challenging the management's story and keep asking yourself if you would invest in the stock at today's prices and with today's prospects.

Another type of behavioral bias is the **anchoring bias**: it is often mentally difficult for an investor to sell a stock at a loss. Therefore, all too often the decision is made to hold on to a stock that has a loss of 10% or even 20%, and sell when you reach the break-even point. This is a ridiculous idea: you either believe in the company and its prospects, or you don't. And need to come to an estimation of the "intrinsic value" of the stock with all knowledge today. The price you specifically paid a couple of days, weeks, or months ago is completely irrelevant. The only thing that matters is your current estimation of the intrinsic value, with all the knowledge of today. But all too often, it proves difficult to cut losses, and sell at a small loss. Always remember that it is better to sell at a small loss than to wait 'til you have a bigger one.

Discussing all types of biases is beyond the scope of this book: an entire encyclopedia can be written about all types of biases.

Just to highlight two of our favorites:

- ▸ The G. I. Joe fallacy: the tendency to think that knowing about a cognitive bias is enough to overcome it.
- ▸ The fallacy fallacy: the tendency to think that, because an argument contains a logical fallacy, its conclusion must be false.

Chapter Summary

Selling is one of the most difficult – and an often underexposed – aspect of investing. In this chapter, the following recommendations were made:

- If the original investment case is not true anymore, sell the stock. (Cut your losses.)

- Don't use stop-loss orders. But redo your homework if a stock drops in value without you knowing the reason behind it.

- Sell a stock if your estimation for its fair value is reached or exceeded. (Don't be too greedy!)

- Negative earnings revisions often come in threes. Sell, especially if the original guidance was expected to be conservative.

- Don't be in a rush to "buy at the bottom" after negative earnings revision.

- Be attentive for red flags such as (soft or hard) accounting manipulations, ERP updates, leadership changes, significant insider selling, or unfaithful management behavior.

And be careful and avoid behavioral biases as much as humanly possible.

CHAPTER 12
Portfolio Construction

> *"I asked my portfolio optimizer to reduce risk. It suggested staying in bed and avoiding the stock market entirely."*
>
> - UNKNOWN

The previous sections discussed how to detect good companies and how to select which stocks to buy. But how many stocks should a portfolio contain? And how to determine the weights of each individual position?

Welcome to the field of portfolio construction and portfolio optimization. And welcome to another overintellectualized field in finance. Hundreds, if not thousands, of papers dedicated to various aspects of portfolio optimization have been published over the last decades. The research basically started with the pathbreaking work of Markowitz in 1952, who derived an *"optimal"* rule for allocating wealth across risky assets based on **mean-variance optimization**. Unfortunately, his technique produces extreme weights that fluctuate substantially over time, and **performs poorly out of sample**. Which is not surprising: the theory suggests that both the mean return and the variance of stocks are not only known, but are also constant over time. In reality, obviously this is not the case.

- Merton (1980) showed in his paper that *"a very long time series of data is required in order to estimate expected returns precisely."* (In our opinion, a more correct statement would be that returns are neither known beforehand, nor constant over time...)
- On average, the variance of [the variance of stocks] is actually about twice the size of the variance of a stock itself. So instead of making the assumption that the variance of a stock is static over time, a better assumption would be to state that the price of a stock is static over time. But that would make the whole investing exercise a bit superfluous...

// PORTFOLIO CONSTRUCTION

One therefore advocates not to overintellectualize the exercise of portfolio construction. And especially avoid complex calculations based on unfulfilled assumptions. Our favorite paper in this research area is titled *"Optimal versus naïve diversification: How inefficient is the 1/N portfolio strategy?"* (DeMiguel, Garlappi and Uppal), published in 2007 by Oxford University Press. It compares the performance of 14 models of mean-variance portfolio optimization models on 8 different datasets and comes to the conclusion that the equal weight portfolio actually showed the best out-of-sample performance. Or, as they describe it: *"allocation mistakes caused by using the 1/N weights can turn out to be smaller than the error caused by using weights from an optimizing model with inputs that have been estimated with error"*...

In theory, portfolio optimization works perfectly. In practice, the market just laughs at these theories. That said, it is undeniable that diversifying a portfolio by increasing the number of stocks does help reduce its overall risk. However, the benefits of diversification diminish as the portfolio becomes more diversified—the marginal risk reduction from adding one more stock decreases over time. Moreover, because all stocks are, to some extent, influenced by the broader economy, there will always be a level of **systematic risk** (or "market risk") that no amount of diversification can eliminate. Thus, without wanting to overintellectualize on the exact numbers, the "risk" (volatility) of a portfolio follows the following pattern:

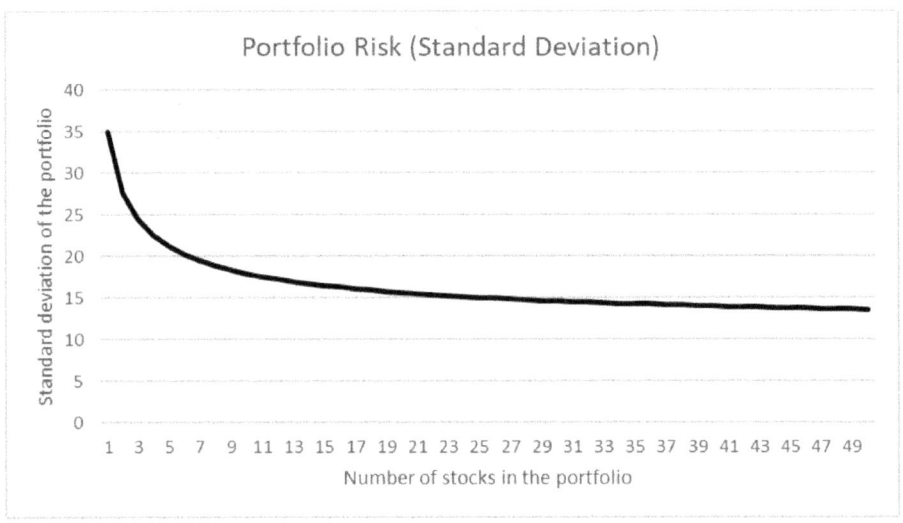

The question remains: how many stocks does the "perfect" portfolio contain, and how large should each of these positions be? Once again: it depends... on your situation personal situation, risk tolerance, and goals.

Maximizing returns

If your goal is to maximize your chances for an exceptional performance regardless of the risks involved, the best way is to have a very concentrated portfolio. The perfect example of this is Elon Musk. He went all-in on PayPal. Then he used the proceeds and went all-in on Tesla. And SpaceX. He borrowed against each of those positions to buy Twitter/X, et cetera. Another example—one you might not expect to have lots of similarities with Elon Musk—is Charlie Munger. At times he wasn't too afraid to put his entire net worth in a concentrated portfolio of only three stocks. And if you are as smart and business savvy as Charlie (or Elon, for that matter), investing in a very concentrated portfolio of your prime picks might indeed be the best idea in order to maximize your returns. Why diversify into "second best ideas" if you can go all-in on your very best one?

However, for most of us, mere mortals, this is a terrible idea. Not only can we be wrong sometimes, which can have disastrous consequences with such concentrated portfolios. But even if we are right, the stock market might "pretend" that we are wrong for an extended period of time. If you are the type of investor who loses sleep, feels stressed, or is tempted to make impulsive, suboptimal decisions when facing a paper loss, this strategy could end up being disastrous, even if you managed to successfully choose the best companies in the market in the first place. So depending on your skills as an analyst[41], your risk tolerance, and susceptibility to behavioral biases, your optimal portfolio should either be more concentrated, or more diversified.

Avoid diworsification

On the other end of the spectrum, there are investors buying every stock they see. Diversification is great, but if you diversify into 300 stocks, you might as well just buy an index fund and take a nap. Which can also be a valid strategy. (Just keep

---

[41] Be realistic, and avoid the overconfidence bias! 😊

// PORTFOLIO CONSTRUCTION

an eye on the diversification of the index, as explained in the box below.) However, given that you already made it this far in this book—without falling asleep—one can assume your ambition is to pick stocks and try to outperform the index.

For most stock pickers, the ideal portfolio consists, roughly, **between 20 and 35 stocks**. This should be sufficient to diversify almost all idiosyncratic risk away. But is concentrated enough to let each position have a meaningful impact if the stock would double, become a four-bagger, or a 10Xer. However, make sure there is a sufficient spread in the type of exposure: to reduce the risk of your portfolio, **a decent sector spread is necessary**.

> ### Buying index trackers: a diversified portfolio?
>
> At first glance, one might assume that index funds offer broad diversification. After all, they provide exposure to hundreds or even thousands of stocks—from the **S&P 500** (which includes 500 companies) to the **Russell 3000** (with 3,000 stocks), and the **Wilshire 5000** (make a guess... Nope! Containing 3,403 stocks[42]!!). However, these large numbers can create a misleading sense of diversification.
>
> Due to the market-cap-weighted structure of most major indices, a handful of the largest companies dominate the overall portfolio. Even in the broadest index, the Wilshire 5000, the top 10 holdings account for more than 30% of the fund's total weight. So the concentration risk is actually a lot higher than one might think by just looking at the number of constituents in the index. And while these concentration levels are not necessarily problematic, it is important to notice that the top six stocks—Apple, Nvidia, Microsoft, Amazon, Meta Platforms, and Alphabet—make up over 25% of the index, and are all tech-related companies.

---

[42] The Wilshire 5000 Total Market Index originally included all publicly traded U.S. stocks, and when it was launched in 1974, it had close to 5,000 stocks—hence the name. However, over time, the number of stocks in the index has dropped below 5,000. Because of M&A, bankruptcies, delisting, and more companies staying in private hands for longer these days...

This concentration means that despite holding thousands of stocks, many index funds are significantly tilted toward a few dominant players, particularly in the tech sector. Investors seeking true diversification should be mindful of this imbalance and consider complementing their portfolio with other asset classes or investment strategies.

How to assign weights to your positions

After determining how many stocks to buy, the next question becomes: how to assign weights to them? Also here, one would suggest a pragmatic approach: **assign weights between 1% and 5% to most of your stocks**. A position above 5% can cause too much damage if your investment case ends up being wrong. A position of less than 1% on the other hand is too small to make a meaningful difference in the returns of your investment portfolio. And be honest: if you want to invest less than 1% of your net worth in a certain stock, are you really convinced of its quality and potential?

Some other guidelines:

- The more upside potential you see, the higher the weight you should assign to this stock.
- Companies where the debt level is at the upper end of the acceptable range are riskier, in the sense that things could go very wrong if the economy turns sour. Therefore, assign a bit more moderate weights to these stocks.
- Keep an eye on sector spreads. If you want to invest in Adidas, Skechers and Crocs at the same time, don't give each of them 5% exposure. Don't let the exposure to the same subsector (in this case: shoes) *run* too high.
- The same reasoning counts for companies that are clients or suppliers from each other. If one sees a sector slowdown, probably the other will also suffer headwinds. So keep the weights of correlated stocks limited.
- Stocks of which the exposure is completely different than everything else in the portfolio can be assigned a slightly higher weight. E.g. an undertaker is probably not that correlated to the Adidas/Skechers/Crocs trio. So in this

// PORTFOLIO CONSTRUCTION

hypothetical example, a company like Service Corporation International—if deemed worth buying—can receive a slightly higher weight than what you would warrant based on its upside potential alone.

Chapter Summary

▸ Portfolio optimization often gets overintellectualized. But most theories are based on mathematical theories for which the prerequisites and assumptions are not fulfilled.

▸ A portfolio containing 20 – 35 stocks, with weights between 1% and 5%, strikes a good balance between diversification without *diworsification*. The more risk tolerant you are, the more concentrated your portfolio may be.

▸ Overweigh stocks where you see the highest upside potential, and the stocks that are the least correlated to the rest of the portfolio. Underweigh stocks with high debt levels, or with strong correlations to other stocks in the portfolio.

CHAPTER 13

How to Select a Fund?

> *"Choosing a fund based on past performance is like driving using only the rearview mirror. Great for knowing where you've been, terrible for knowing where you're going."*
>
> - RONALD H. MUHLENKAMP

I hope this book sparked your enthusiasm for learning more about investments and, if you're not an investor already, to start investing in the first place. You can do this yourself by actively scanning the markets and analyzing businesses, as you now have the tools to pick the right stocks. Alternatively, you can buy a fund or ETF. Important to note is that one doesn't have to exclude the other. A good investment strategy can be to put part of your net worth into a low-cost index fund or ETF that performs (almost) in line with the broader market. And to use another part of your means to perform some active stock picking, or to invest in an actively managed fund that tries to outperform the markets.

Why are people buying funds?

Creating a portfolio of handpicked stocks is basically a full-time job. There are thousands of stocks to choose from. The price at which you can buy or sell them changes daily. And the performance of each of these companies is reported quarterly. Furthermore, to end up with a good portfolio, diversification and risk management need to be considered. And it does not suffice to perform this exercise just once. Even for a buy-and-hold investor, it is important to keep track of your portfolio, and to see how each company is performing.

It also takes more than just following the companies in your portfolio. Competitors need to be followed up too, as well as companies that are on a watchlist that might become a part of the portfolio if the price and the time are right. So creating and following up a stock portfolio is a very interesting, but also a very time consuming activity, for which skill and discipline are required. Therefore, a lot of investors opt not to do the job themselves, but to outsource this task to a professional portfolio manager by buying an equity fund.

How to select an equity fund?

As a portfolio manager myself, it is not uncommon to be asked questions on how to select a fund. And while the question is easy, the answer is not. This might sound incredible, but there are more funds than stocks. So in a certain way, buying funds instead of stocks shifts the problem—from choosing the right stocks to choosing the right funds—instead of solving it. Or at least for the initial selection. Because once selected, an investment in a fund needs a lot less follow-up compared to a portfolio of individual stocks.

So how can one select a fund? It is important to keep in mind that the top performing fund in one year seldomly is among the best performing ones the year after. So fund-hopping, or frequently switching towards the fund that performed best over the most recent period, is a fools game in which you end up a loser more often than not. And on top of that, you might face considerable costs when switching. From transaction costs and entry fees, over taxes in the form of stamp duties, or in the form of capital gains taxes, depending on the jurisdiction in which you are living. So my recommendation would be to thoroughly do the research beforehand, pick a fund, and stick with it for the long term, with the sole exception being if something outrageous happens. E.g. shake-ups in the management team of your fund, or performance lacking for an extended period of time (years, not months).

In what follows, a number of topics are touched upon, to take into consideration when opting for buying a fund. Expect no clear-cut answers on a specific fund though: there is no holy grail, nor a "one-size-fits-all" solution. Everything depends on your own situation and preferences. You are the only one who can take those decisions for yourself. This chapter merely provides a proverbial coat rack that can be used to guide you through the decision-making process.

Active versus Passive

One of the first decisions to be made is whether you want an actively managed fund, or a passive index fund.

In an actively managed fund, the portfolio manager makes a selection of stocks that, according to his or her insights and expertise, will perform better than the market as a whole. The fund actively tries to exploit market movements, by buying and selling under- and overvalued stocks while trying to obtain a higher return.

In a passively managed fund, the investor buys the entire index. In that case, the stock selection is not made by the portfolio manager, but rather it is outsourced towards the formulas used by the index providers (often S&P or MSCI). In most cases these indices are "market cap weighted," which means that a larger chunk of your money is invested in larger companies, and a lesser part in smaller companies. You will invest twice as much money in a company that is twice as large (measured by its market cap). Regardless of valuation multiples, future outlook, or other company specifics. Investors in these funds assume that the stock market is more or less efficiently priced, and they save themselves the effort to form a vision about stocks or stock prices. They just buy the entire market.

The advantage of passive funds is that management fees are generally very low. There is no follow-up of the stock selection, and the number of transactions is also extremely low: Once every quarter or so there might be a rebalancing, in which certain stocks enter or exit the index, but that's about it. On the other hand, this means the investor will never outperform the market as a whole. And that a relatively large chunk of the money is invested in the largest companies of the index. Furthermore, the more expensive a company, the more stocks a market-cap weighted fund will buy, because of its market-weighting mechanism. Which, at the same time, has the advantage of limiting the number of transactions needed:

- in an "equal weighted portfolio" every time stock prices fluctuate, the weight of the different stocks in the portfolio fluctuate, and thus trading is needed to rebalance: what increased in value now has a higher weight, and needs to be sold. The relative laggards are now underweight, and need to be bought. So in principle every day additional transactions are needed.

- In a "market cap weighted portfolio," if a stock increases in value, its market cap increases, and thus the weight to be attributed increases equally. So there is no need to rebalance or transact.

In general, fewer transactions is better, as trading costs can become a true subtractor of fund performance. So if you opt for a passive ETF, market cap weighted ones might be preferable.

Diversification – Regions & Sectors

A second choice that is to be made is, in which region do you want to invest? Is your focus on buying worldwide stocks? Or do you prefer a focus on American or European stocks? Or do you want to risk your luck by buying stocks in emerging markets in Asia or South America? Or do you fancy a bit of nationalism, by investing in stocks of the country you live in?

The obvious advantage of investing in worldwide stocks is diversification. By investing in a very broad range of companies and regions, specific risks are diversified away. A disadvantage is that foreign currency risk is taken, and that geopolitical risks can have a larger impact on the performance of your portfolio. Those risks are even exacerbated when investing in emerging markets. Internal political regime switches can have an outsized impact on the return of your fund, and in the worst case a number of *your* companies can get nationalized. Or additional taxes can be levied, up till a level that makes your stock worthless. On the other hand, those regions generally have a slightly higher economic growth rate compared to the United States, Europe or Japan.

Investments in companies closer to home have the advantage of being easier to follow up or read something about in the local press. They are thus generally a bit better known to the investor community in your region.

Similar remarks can be made in relation to sectors: are you looking for exposure to a specific sector, or do you want a diversified investment across the entire market? And what does the rest of your portfolio look like? E.g. if you are an engineer with an interest in financial markets (and some spare time), it can be an option to do some active stock picking of industrial, technological and even some consumer product companies. And use passive funds in real estate and pharmaceutical companies, assuming the engineer has less knowledge and affinity to dive deeper into the market dynamics in those sectors. For someone active in a medical profession, it might be the other way around.

Costs and cost structure, and the tax man

Obviously, costs are also an important consideration. A fund with high fees is like a slow leak in your boat: you won't notice at first, but eventually, you're sinking.

Some funds charge an **entry fee** of 2%-3% of assets. This is very high, and ensures you already start with a disadvantage. Try to negotiate this fee away, *at all costs*.

Next, the **management fees** are also an important one. These should be below 2% in my opinion, no matter how good the portfolio manager is. Charging a management fee of 2% means the portfolio needs to beat the benchmark by 2% per year, just to break even after costs, which is a very hard task to do. This is also the main reason most portfolio managers fail to beat their benchmark on an after-cost basis.

Third, is there a **performance fee**? Potentially with a high-water mark? For example, the fund might charge fees of 10%-20% of the outperformance it generates compared to an index, or above an absolute return goal. E.g. if that goal is 6%, and the fund returns 10%, then there is a 4% outperformance, of which 20% or thus 80 basis points are charged as fees. In that case the return for the investor equals 9.2%. So performance fees also eat up part of your returns, but only when the performance of the fund is above the high-water mark.

There are advantages and disadvantages, but in general it is preferable to choose funds with a relatively low management fee, and an acceptable performance fee, because it aligns the incentives between the investor and the manager. As a high-level guideline, and in our personal opinion, a 1% management fee and 10% performance fee strikes a good balance, as it aligns the interests of the investment company with the one of the investor.

- With a zero-management fee, the investment company doesn't earn anything in years with a bad performance. While this might seem well-deserved—bad performance shouldn't be incentivized—it may lead to the manager taking outrageous risks in the closing weeks of a year: The manager gets incentivized to take coin flips. Heads—the managing company gets to charge a fee. Tails—it's the investor who loses money, not the managing company. A (somewhat small) management fee ensures that part of the income of the investment company is based on the Assets under Management (AuM). Which means those coinflips do have a negative impact on its income: all actions that decrease the AuM mean that the management fee is taken from a lower AuM amount, which translates into less income.

- The performance fee ensures that the focus of the company is directed towards obtaining decent investment returns. This sounds obvious, but if there is no performance fee, the main incentive of the investment company is mainly to manage a large pot of money, regardless of the performance. Marketing might become more important than actual investment returns…

- If the performance fee is too high, there are again incentives to take huge risks with your money. If they pay off, the investment company strikes gold and charges a hefty performance fee. If it doesn't, the loss is on you, and the company might close the door and start another fund and try the same trick again. Too many (but not all) hedge funds have this trick up their sleeves.

Thus, a good balance, that aligns incentives as good as possible, should be sought after. As the late Charlie Munger would say: *"Show me the incentives, and I'll show you the outcome."*

Extra points are awarded to investment companies in which the company and its managers have most of their own money invested in the funds as well, alongside client money. This aligns the incentives of management and clients even further and should be a best practice in the industry. All too often this doesn't happen, though. Especially at large bank institutions, it is sad to see how low the percentage of personnel is that actually invests in the own investment products of the institution they work for. That might tell you something about the quality of the products they deliver…

The Portfolio Managers

In case you opt for an actively managed fund, it is definitely worth your time to look up who is actually managing your fund. Obviously, you want to know about the reputation of the investment company you are entrusting your money to. But it is also worth looking a little further and checking the person managing your fund. We are not talking about that cute sales representative, but about the fund manager who is actually calling the shots in your portfolio and making the daily investment decisions. Is that person someone with yearslong experience, or can you expect some youthful enthusiasm? And for how long has the fund already been managed by the same people? Funds in which the portfolio manager changes yearly can be a reason for doubt. Is there sufficient continuity and vision in the investment strategy? Or are a whole bunch of transaction costs generated every time the portfolio manager changes, because he or she wants to put his/her own mark on the portfolio?

And how many funds are being managed by that person? If the portfolio manager is responsible for another 20 different funds, next to yours, you can certainly question whether sufficient attention is being given to follow up your portfolio.

Conversely, if the fund is "managed by committee", there are consequences on what can be expected. If a group of 10 people needs to gather and agree on every decision, one is ensured of two things: a slow decision-making process in which decisions always lag the markets. And a more diversified portfolio with a less outspoken positioning, because the entire group needs to agree with the final decision.

Last but not least, the communication of the investment company is important. Are they openly disclosing what happens in the fund, and why? Or is communication limited to the legal minimum required by law? Is the portfolio manager transparent, or is there no response in the desired way at times of market crashes?

Historical Returns

One ends this chapter by kicking in an open door: how where the historical returns of the fund you are considering investing in? Often this is the very first, and sometimes the only, thing potential investors pay attention to. And while past returns are never a guarantee for the future, the opposite is often true: historical non-performance in the past may be a leading indicator of future underperformance... It is however important to nuance the importance of past performances. It is very useful to know the past performance, but simply sorting the list of funds by historical return, from high to low, and picking the top one, is shortsighted. Especially if taken over short time periods.

Other useful questions to ask are:

- is the portfolio manager still in place? If the good track record was set by a previous manager, who retired or switched jobs, that history might be less relevant for the future performance of the fund.
- How much risk was taken to obtain that result?
- What is the current valuation of the companies in which the fund is invested in?
- How many transactions have been executed lately?

If the fund used to invest in undervalued stocks, and those got more expensive to the point that they are not undervalued anymore but are still present in the portfolio. Then you are buying a fund with an excellent track record, but you enter the investment at high valuations. If, on the other hand, the fund monetized some of the now overvalued stocks, and invested the proceeds in other, undervalued companies, the situation could be completely different.

Chapter Summary

There is no "one-size-fits-all" when selecting funds. Keep the following topics in mind when making your personal selection:

- **Active vs. Passive Funds**: Active funds aim to outperform the market but have higher fees; passive funds track an index with lower costs but won't beat the market. A mix of both can be a solid strategy.

- **Diversification**: Choose between global, regional, or sector-specific funds. Global funds reduce specific risks but introduce currency and geopolitical exposure.

- **Costs Matter**: Avoid high entry fees, prioritize low management fees (<2%), and ensure performance fees align manager incentives with investor interests.

- **Fund Manager Selection**: Look for stability, experience, and transparency. Avoid funds with frequent leadership changes or excessive committee oversight.

- **Historical Returns in Context**: Past performance isn't everything. Assess risk levels, valuation, and management consistency before investing.

- **Long-Term Commitment**: Avoid fund-hopping; research thoroughly, choose wisely, and stick with a fund unless major red flags arise.

CHAPTER 14

Closing Remarks

> *"A conclusion is simply the place where you got tired of thinking."*
>
> – ARTHUR BLOCH

Throughout this book, we have explored the core principles of intelligent investing, by moving beyond market noise, emotional biases, and short-term distractions to focus on what truly matters. From understanding different investment philosophies to challenging the traditional Efficient Market Hypothesis, we've seen how successful investors rely on independent thinking rather than blindly following conventional wisdom.

We have examined the hallmarks of the perfect company, the importance of valuation—including the pitfalls of a number of popular valuation metrics—and the critical role of capital allocation, mergers & acquisitions, and sustainable growth on stock returns. And as a business does not exist in isolation, we also expanded our view to assess sector and regional dynamics, as well as the quality of management and the importance and impact of other shareholders. Understanding these layers allows investors to make better-informed decisions and avoid costly pitfalls.

But investing is not just about buying great companies. It's also about knowing when to sell, and about how to construct a well-balanced portfolio that withstands volatility and aligns with one's financial goals. We also briefly touched the topic of equity fund selection, which can be almost as challenging as stock picking itself.

If there's one overarching lesson, it's this: the best investors think for themselves. They don't simply follow trends, mimic peers, or chase short-term gains. They embrace challenges, welcome opposing viewpoints, and continuously refine their approach.

/// CLOSING REMARKS

The market will always be noisy: full of distractions, speculation, and misleading narratives. But beyond that noise lies real value, waiting to be uncovered by those who take the time to look deeper. The ability to cut through the chaos, focus on fundamentals, and stay disciplined is what separates great investors from the rest.

I hope this book has provided you with valuable insights and a structured approach to investing. But remember, learning never stops. The market is constantly evolving, and so should your understanding of it. Stay curious, remain skeptical, and always be willing to challenge your own assumptions. Because the mind is like a parachute, it only works when it is open.

At the end of the day, investing is not just about numbers—it's about perspective, patience, and independent thought. And about daring to take actions and decisions based on ones own belief, even if the rest of the world seems to have a different opinion. If you can master this, you will truly be investing beyond the noise.

Good Luck!

Jens Verbrugge,
Equity Analyst & Portfolio Manager

> "Lots of people know what to do, but few people actually do what they know. Knowing is not enough! You must take action."
>
> – TONY ROBINSON

ACKNOWLEDGEMENTS

This book grew out of fifteen years of following financial markets and analyzing stocks. My dad Joost gave me my first book about investing when I was 13 years of age, and the interest was awakened. Thank you for everything, dad!

I also want to thank my colleagues Kris Hermie, Patrick Millecam and Wouter Verlinden for their valuable insight and inspiration and for helping me learn the ropes of equity analysis. And to Koen Hoffman for trusting me and the team throughout the ups and downs inherent to investing in noisy markets.

Also a shout-out to Laurent Lamblin, who deserves an explicit thank-you for enlightening me on the need to focus on quality and growth alongside price, amongst hundreds of other valuable lessons and laughs.

A heartfelt thank you to Ashley Emma, for the editing work, and to Saqib Arshad, for the help with formatting this book. And to Celine Deschepper, Jos Callens and Kristoff Van Houte for pre-reading and for delivering valuable suggestions and improvement, all of which contributed to enhancing the depth and quality of this work.

www.ingramcontent.com/pod-product-compliance
Lightning Source LLC
LaVergne TN
LVHW061613070526
838199LV00078B/7263